Woven
Voices

Woven Voices

3 Generations of
Puertorriqueña Poets
Look at Their
American Lives

Anita Vélez-Mitchell
Gloria Vando
Anika Paris

edited by
Linda Rodriguez

Scapegoat Press
Kansas City, Missouri

Scapegoat Press
P.O. Box 401962
Kansas City, Missouri 64141
www.scapegoat-press.com

Library cataloguing-in-publication data is available.

ISBN 978-0-9791291-4-8

ACKNOWLEDGMENTS

Anita Velez-Mitchell

"A Fragrant Meal" first appeared in *In the Black/In the Red: Poems of Profit & Loss* (Helicon Nine Editions).

"Hard Covers" first appeared in *Poetic Vioces Without Borders II* (Gival Press).

"The Milky Way" first appeared in *Chance of a Ghost* (Helicon Nine Editions).

"My Will" first appeared in *The Kansas City Star*.

"Marzo" / "March" first appeared in *Primavida: A Calendar of Love* (Mairena Press).

"Qué Tío" (translation of "Cry Uncle") first appeared in *Ejército de rosas* (Revista Boreales).

Gloria Vando

"Bicoastal: The Sell Date on My Life Has Expired" first appeared in *Poetic Voices Without Borders* (Gival Press).

"Borinquen" first appeared in *Poetic Voices Without Borders* (Gival Press).

"Cry Uncle" first appeared in *Promesas: Geography of the Impossible* (Arte Público Press).

"The Day Began as Usual" from "Heroes and Villains," a poem in three parts, first appeared in *In the Black/In the Red: Poems of Profit & Loss* (Helicon Nine Editions).

"Empty Nester" first appeared in *I-70 Review*.

"Global Warming" first appeared in *presentmagazine.com*.

"Growing Into Lilac" first appeared in *The Movable Nest* (Helicon Nine Editions).

"Guernica" first appeared in *Cortland Review*.

"Legend of the Flamboyan" appeared in *Promesas: Geography of the Impossible* (Arte Público Press).

"My 90-Year-Old Father and My Husband Discuss Their Trips to the Moon" first appeared in *New Letters*.

"Noche de Ronda" was published in *Shadows & Supposes* (Arte Público Press).

"Nuyorican Lament" appeared in *Promesas: Geography of the Impossible* (Arte Público Press).

"Out of Sync" first appeared in *Spillway Magazine*.

An earlier version of "The Shape of Things" appeared as "Late Autumn" in *River Styx*.

"A String of Pearls" first appeared in *Tar River Poetry*.

"Wind Chill Factor" first appeared in *Luna: a journal of poetry and translation*, vol. 6 and was later published in *Shadows & Supposes* (Arte Público Press).

Anika Paris

"On Buying Our First House Moments Before the Mortgage Crisis" first appeared in *In the Black/In the Red: Poems of Profit and Loss*, (Helicon Nine Editions).

"Border Line" first appeared in *Poetic Voices Without Borders 2* (Gival Press).

"Synthesis" first appeared in *Spillway Magazine*.

"Widowed Heart" first appeared in *The Kansas City Star.*.

"August Eve" first appeared in *Chance of a Ghost: An Anthology of Ghost Poems* (Helicon Nine Editions).

"Leap Frog" first appeared in *The Mom Egg*.

Woven Voices

INTRODUCTION

This is not your usual book of poetry. It was designed to be a different kind of poetic experience—a conversation of poetry among three very different but truly related poets, Anita Vélez-Mitchell, grandmother and mother, Gloria Vando, mother and daughter, and Anika Paris, daughter and granddaughter. Therefore, a little background becomes necessary.

I first became friends with Gloria Vando over twenty-five years ago, but it was only a few years ago that I became fully aware that she was the middle of a three-generation sandwich of talented poets, along with her mother, Anita Vélez-Mitchell, and her daughter, Anika Paris. Ever since then, however, I have wanted to gather those poetic voices and braid them into one whole, to bring them into conversation with each other about their lives.

These three generations span geography, also, with Anita born and raised in Vieques, Puerto Rico, and moving to the continental United States to live for most of her life, Gloria born and raised in the United States, mostly by grandparents still mentally resident in Puerto Rico, and Anika born and raised in the United States by American-born parents. Each generation has had a different experience as a woman of Puerto Rican descent living in the United States.

I wanted to capture those three different but related experiences in conversation with each other—about their lives, about their countries and sense of home, about their family, about their experiences of each other and their relationships with each other. Many of Vélez-Mitchell's poems were originally written in Spanish and have been translated to English by either herself or Vando, and some of Vando's poems have been translated into Spanish by either herself or Vélez-Mitchell. I wanted to provide these poems in both languages since the bilingual experience is an essential part of these writers.

Each woman has a distinctive voice in poetry. Born and

raised in Puerto Rico until she came to New York in early adolescence, Vélez-Mitchell's work is more romantic and traditional with frequent displays of razor-sharp, flirtatious wit. Long a successful and highly regarded actress and dancer, she also writes frequently of the back side of show business, something Vando also remembers from her childhood in several poems. Vando, who was born and raised in New York with frequent visits to the island her family came from, offers the most literary and polished voice with the greatest variety of subject matter, form, and style, while Paris' voice is hipper, more sardonic with great insight and humor.

The work of each woman has been divided among common subjects and placed in relation to work of the other two women, forming a poetic conversation or plática, the poetic equivalent of pulling up a chair and sitting with a cup of tea or coffee to listen to the three generations of women talking together about the important issues of their lives and often laughing together, as well.

The richest of the subjects are home, mothers and daughters, and family. This is hardly surprising since the family these women come from began in Puerto Rico and continues in the United States and the three generations of this family are full of great ambition, talent, and achievement, as well as misunderstanding of, love for, and the desire to be loved by their parents, siblings, and children.

In sharp nostalgia for their complicated familial homeland, both Vando and Vélez-Mitchell write moving poems (in "Legend of the Flamboyán" and "Totém Taíno" respectively) about the history of the encounter between the indigenous inhabitants of the island they called Borinquén and the Spanish conquistadores, which led to the loss of the Taíno's land and independence, slavery, death-dealing illness, and, finally, Taíno mass suicide. In "Totém Taíno," Vélez-Mitchell also writes in sympathetic detail of the leaders of the Taíno—caciques—and their sacrifices for their people. She has researched these indigenous ancestors and written an opera libretto, "Temple of the Souls," dealing with the Taíno, which premiered in New York City in December 2011. Anika composed the music and Lorca Peress, Vando's other daughter, produced and directed it.

Vélez-Mitchell and Vando also engage repeatedly with the privilege of their ancestors and aunts and uncles in a bittersweet tone that recognizes the injustice at its base and the damage it causes its recipients, especially seen in Vélez-Mitchell's "Miramar, Puerto

Rico." Vando, in particular, can be scornful toward her elderly, wealthy (or once-wealthy) relatives still resident in Puerto Rico when she goes to visit them as a young girl who is growing to maturity in the freer atmosphere of New York City. Paris, on the other hand, writes in the poignant "Border Line" of the gap between her friends' and her American privilege and the residents of a poor Mexican village, "... catering to us like royalty/ filling our cups till they overflow/..." and the disparity between her American friends' delight and her own discomfort.

In "Birthright" and "Nuyorican Lament," Vando looks at her own displacement from Puerto Rico as a Nuyorican, "... a trespasser in my own past,/ tracing a faint ancestral theme/ far back..." while Vélez-Mitchell asserts that Puerto Rico remembers her as she does her first home—"... Though my 'r's no longer roll/ the island will nurture my spirit..."

In "Leap Frog," Paris, born in this country and raised in Texas and Kansas, discusses the politics of color in her family—"My mother, a fair-skinned Puerto Rican, told me/ she married my father hoping to have exotic children/ Her sister Jane told me she always felt like the dark one/ I, blonde and blue-eyed, only wanted Jordache jeans/..."—and both the alienation from and longing for the ancestral homeland and culture—"We third-generationers get the watered-down/ version of our grandparents' stories/ the language barrier widening in time/ ...while the coqui's song fades in the distance/...I want to go back to where I've never been/ and sing along."

Not surprisingly for women whose personal and family histories include such displacements, the largest section in the book is called simply HOME. However, this section is not devoted entirely to dual longings for the ancestral home and for a true sense of belonging to the current home. There is humor and joy here, as well. Paris simultaneously rejoices in a new dwelling and pokes fun at her lack of foresight in "On Buying Our First House Moments Before the Mortgage Crisis," ultimately coming down on the side of the ancient desire to possess one's own home. Vélez-Mitchell exults in the sense of homecoming to New York City's rhythms and to her own body that her dance lessons with a well-known jazz dancer provide her, while Vando, in "Bicoastal: The Sell Date on My Life Has Expired," ponders reaching a period in her life where she travels repeatedly from California to Kansas to New York and back again, always finding that what she needs is in one of the other places and waking after travel to walk into walls and closets.

The relationship between mother and adult daughter is always fraught with tensions, and never more than in cases of ambitious, talented mothers and ambitious, talented daughters. In the section on mothers and daughters, Vélez-Mitchell, Vando, and Paris deal honestly and openly with some of these tensions, which are not often considered from both sides, let alone from the following generation, as well. Consequently, we have poems written from the persona of the young daughter hurt by her mother's need to make a living and build a career, which the child sees as abandonment, along with poems in the viewpoint of the adult daughter in an accepting, loving relationship with that same mother. Vélez-Mitchell's "To My Mother, Lucila Rieckehoff" gives us a glimpse of the unreconciled longing for the absent mother that begins this long line of maternal touch-and-go. Vando's heartbreaking "Islands: Isla Madre, Isla Nena" continues this vein, exchanging Vélez-Mitchell for the grandmother who is the unattainable love object of the former poem. In turn, Vando's touching "Chorus Line" and Paris's "Synthesis" reveal adult daughters making peace with the people that their respective mothers are, the irony being that Paris is speaking of her mother Vando as Vando speaks of her own mother Vélez-Mitchell while Vélez-Mitchell in "Symbol of a Dream" and "Breaking the Silence" deals with her complicated relationship with her youngest daughter (television news anchor Jane Vélez-Mitchell) and the love she feels for her.

The conversation around mothers and daughters is not all recrimination and heartbreak, however. Paris's hilarious "Poetic Playground" shows the joy for a precocious young daughter of a flamboyant poet-mother who defended her against morality charges from "... an elementary school teacher and Jesus freak." Vélez-Mitchell in "Keep in Touch" describes the love she has for her daughter, Vando, "...touching love/ through our fingertips..." while Vando in "Insight" expresses her astonishment at her mother's willingness to trust her tiny daughter to a virtual stranger and gratitude for her mother's ability to charm that world-famous eye surgeon into operating on her child's eye.

In the section on family, all three poets discuss and display this remarkable family's achievements and idealistic efforts in politics, music, dance, theatre, the visual arts, poetry, and the art of the perfect café con leche. Paris, however, in "The Bigger Picture" shows how concern for her ailing father brings back memories of "... that Xeroxed black and white copy/ of my grandmother's family portrait/ that we show every Passover/ naming each one killed in the Holocaust/..." as Vando remembers her aunt and her women friends in "A String of Pearls" dancing the lindy "well past the hour of pain..." after "...the war had taken all their men—/ including Uncle Ralph who was in the Navy—/ planting them in strange ports and rain-/ drenched jungles with secret names..." and describes with great affection the tender understanding her husband gives her elderly and failing father in "My 90-Year-Old Father and My Husband Discuss their Trips to the Moon." Paris's funny yet wistful poem, "Baby Depot," dissects the classic situation of the career woman at the end of the twentieth and beginning of the twenty-first centuries—"I'm sitting next to 40/ and still thinking I want a baby/ then I quickly change my mind/ I have no money and no room in my house/I'm not even married / and I think I'm in college...."

This is a family with strong roots in Puerto Rican and Nuyorican political and artistic culture. Puerto Rico, of course, is a part of the United States, and its residents are U.S. citizens. The relationship between Puerto Rico and the United States government has a complicated history, reaching back to its involuntary annexation by the U.S. in 1898 in the Spanish-American War, and is often forgotten—or never really known—by many residents of the continental U.S.

Vando's father and uncle (Vélez-Mitchell's ex-husband and brother) were famous proponents of Puerto Rican independence—famous to Puerto Ricans and Puerto Rican Americans as great patriots, if not elsewhere in the United States. This was brought home to me at the 2010 Associated Writers and Writing Programs national conference in Denver when Vando stood up to read a poem at the One Poem Reading, featuring Latino poets from around the country and co-sponsored by Letras Latinas and the Poetry Foundation. A number of Puerto Rican poets and writers in the audience went wild with applause for her as she walked up to the podium with calls of "Vando!" and "Boricua!" as they had not for other Puerto Rican poets who had read, astonishing the other writers and audience members whose cultural roots lay in Mexico and Central and South America.

Vando writes in "The Mouse That Roared" about her father Erasmo Vando's speech to the United Nations, a futile request for the UN's support for Puerto Rican independence, and in "The Day My Uncle Became a Revolutionary" about her maternal uncle Carlos Vélez-Rieckehoff's moment of conversion to the cause of independence during an infamous massacre of unarmed supporters of independence, which would lead to his arrest and imprisonment later as a revolutionary. In "Cry Uncle," Vando gives a portrait of this same uncle as an aged lion, still untamed, at her son's wedding and the difficult family dynamics within which she's lived her life—"... In the photo my husband later will take,/ my mother will lean toward her brother, he/ toward me, and I, stalwart as a tree,/ try to keep the House of Medina from toppling down..."

Vélez-Mitchell in "Little Girls" and "Sisters" gives us portraits of three sisters growing up in good-natured poverty and of the competition between two of them that eventually ends in respect. In "Wings," she writes of the miracle of flight first found when her uncle Frank flies his plane, something previously seen only in books and newspapers, to Vieques where ten-year-old Vélez-Mitchell goes up into the sky for the first time in her life.

Moving into the section on love, these three voices offer us varying perspectives on different kinds of love relationships. Vélez-Mitchell's poignant "Dreamsong" looks back on a life lived in partnership from the new perspective of a widow—"...Dreaming half/ of a dream/ singing half/ of a song." Paris joins in her grandmother's mourning for a loved one lost to death in "Then Came the Rain"—"... Goodbye, My Love, you've typed/ in the subject box of my email//By the time you read this it'll be too late..." but love is not always sad or tragic. Sometimes it is merely complicated and sometimes funny. Vando negotiates the different views of time that she and her husband of many years hold in "Out of Sync"—"... I am Latina late. He scowls. Fumes./ Wrings his hands. Paces the room. ...," but in the more humorous "On Hearing My Mother Speak Lovingly of Dillinger," Vando contrasts her more practical view of love with Vélez-Mitchell's dreamy, romantic perspective while, in "March," Vélez-Mitchell offers the reader a tongue-in-cheek reverie on herself as an adolescent first awakening to the sexual charms of the boys around her and her own sexual power. In the final poem in this section, "Hardcovers," Vélez-Mitchell sings a love hymn to the number and variety of classic books to be found in the used book stores of New York City—"...How can anyone throw such faithful friends away?/ Friends come in handy when one/ is lonely..."

This book ends with the three women in the long tradition of sitting around the kitchen table telling stories and trying to make sense of the world through the lens of narrative. Vélez-Mitchell, whose career in the arts has been remarkable and whose opera written in her nineties recently debuted in New York, opens with an ironic narrative of her search for "My Fountain of Youth," followed by Vando's account in "Dr. Feelgood" of a questionable injection from a physician to the stars. In "In Perfect Key," Paris writes a nostalgic account of reconnecting with childhood friends and a favorite piece of music, "...reclaiming my youth" while she laughs at the American audience and herself in her spoof of contemporary television, "Reality TV."

Paris shines in this section of the book, offering a delightfully horrific mystery novel in nineteen stanzas in "Meddling Betty," an affectionate portrait of high-spirited, ninety-year-old "Daisy Rae Black"—"'I come all the way from St. Joe, Missouri, to hear jazz'"—and a light-hearted meditation that ranges from God and the Holy Spirit to the clothes dryer's lost socks in "Pondering the Existence of God and Other Things." More seriously, Paris gives her own moving account of a married couple's ordinary morning argument on 9/11, "Widowed Heart."

Vando tenders a hilarious account of her difficulties with airport security and the way Vélez-Mitchell, after having her identity stolen, found an old Screen Actors Guild membership card in one pocket—"... Suddenly she was a persona grata, an aging/ movie queen, and they let her on the flight to L.A./ ... My daughter Anika swears/ that in Los Angeles it's illegal to be over 25,/ have an independent thought, and sport real breasts./ But that all changes once you reach 90. ..."

These stories often have political connotations, as well. Vando's "The 'F' Word" presents a sharp, compelling portrait of the forcible eviction of a decorated veteran and his family from their foreclosed home, and Paris discusses in "Suburban Suicide" the futile attempts many make to barricade themselves from the poverty, despair, and crime they see—"... Just a hiccup north, we're deep in Mexico,/ all the men standing on corners begging for work./ Slightly west, a quiet neighborhood I wouldn't/ want to walk in alone at night. ..." In her powerful "The Day Began As Usual," which is part of a larger poem of hers titled "Heroes and Villains," Vando compares NPR's tribute to Dietrich Bonhoeffer using the words of Arnold Schoenberg's "A Survivor from Warsaw" with meditations on the modern American hatred of the poor, the immigrant, the outsider. In "Stick Figures," Vando marches to protest the wars in Iraq and Afghanistan with both her childhood friend and Paris, and in "Guernica" a needlepoint kit for a replica of that famous painting leads to her weary meditation that moves from the Spanish Civil War to Vietnam to current wars and the obscenity of Picasso's protest against war "...stenciled for dowagers/ to stitch in shades of gray/ while viewing newer wars/ in living color."

However, in "Around the Corner" and "Conspiracy," Vélez-Mitchell identifies dissolution and death as the real concerns. In the end, Vélez-Mitchell has the final say in the book, positing "...poetry,/ a trunkless wild vine/ that would rather lie/ in the hay and look up/ at the stars in lovers' eyes..." as the ideal that will save human souls.

This conversation braiding these poetic voices together offers the reader a rare view into the thought processes and lives of these women writers of separate generations and interconnected lives as they negotiate the immigrant family's constantly shifting concept of home and homeland amid the sometimes frustrating, always nourishing constant of family. The music of these three voices singing sometimes in harmony, sometimes in counterpoint, creates a dramatic story that draws in the reader and enriches and enlarges the reader's world.

Linda Rodriguez
Kansas City, Missouri
February 2, 2012

Home

HOMING

The land has a memory too.
Borinquen bemoans my
absence...I sense it blue.

Were I to return to my island
the sky, a multi-tinted hue,
would holler, "I missed you too."

The sea, undulating rhythmically,
will play my favorite melody:
Preciosa te llaman las olas
del mar que te bañan....

The sun from its radiant shell
will shout, "You look so well!"

Fiesta colors will dance for me
with offerings of luscious fruits
from earth and sea. They
still enthrall my memory.

Though my "r"s no longer roll,
the island will nurture my spirit
and smile or scowl or scold,
"Don't forget your mother tongue."

¡Caramba! ¡Si hasta sueño en español!
Yes, I even *dream* in Spanish!

I know where I belong.
I am limned with you in
thought-time, Borinquen—
wherever I go.

Though I might never breathe
your blissful air again,
my Edenic homeland, I know
you will welcome my soul.

Gloria Vando

BORINQUEN

estoy
sumamente
lejos de ti
lejos del *tiqui tiqui*
de las maracas que se reían
con tus llamadas
en días de fruto
en horas de canto

lejos del *tun tu cu tun*
de tu corazón
que acompañaba el *tiqui tiqui*
de las maracas que se burlaban
de tus llamadas
en días de luto
en horas de espanto

y tú encerrado en el timbre
del coquí
en el llanto de palmas
en el son son son
de tu isla perdida
llamando a tu encanto
llamando a tu vida
con el *tiqui tiqui*
de las maracas
y el *tun tu cu tun*
de tu corazón
llamando
llamando
llamando

LEGEND OF THE FLAMBOYÁN

1.

It was a good old-fashioned
victory—no massacres, no fires,
no children gunned down
in the streets of day,
no cameras to point a finger
and say *he* did it, or *they*;
it was calm, it was civilized—
they emerged from the ocean
and claimed their paradise.

From the rain forest, naked and
trembling beneath scheffleras
and figs, perched like purple
gallinules among the low branches
of the jacarandas, the Taínos
watched the iron-clad strangers
wade awkwardly ashore, their
banners staking out their land.

Chief Agüeybaná watched also,
the gold *guanín* glinting
on his chest like a target.
Who were these intruders and what
were they doing on this island?
Could they be cannibals like
the Caribes? Could they be gods?
Their bodies glistened like stars,
their eyes like the sea.

The Taínos met and argued
well into the night, weighing
the pros and cons of strategies—
if these were gods, to ignore them
might incite their wrath,
to fight them might invite death.
Best to rejoice then and welcome
the silver giants to Boriquén.

The Spaniards responded by
taking first their freedom,
then their land, then
using them as human picks to dig
for gold—gold for the crown,
gold for the holy faith,
gold for the glory of Spain.

2.

The darkness of the mines
consumed them, sapped
their laughter, their song,
locking them into perpetual night.
The women withdrew, drew in,
their hearts hard
against the longing they saw
in the strangers' eyes—
not to look, not to be seen—
they bowed their heads, folded
into themselves like secrets
whispered only in the safety
of brown arms.

3.

A wrecked vessel washed ashore
at Guajataca. The children raced
down to the beach looking
for treasures, looking under
torn sails, beneath coiled ropes,
turning over loosened boards,
and suddenly—a hand, then a face,
the skin pale and mottled, the eyes
staring up at them, opaque
like a fish, the color of the sea.

Something dead. Something *ungodly.*

The island echoed their cries.

That night the Taínos planned
carefully, knowing—
like those at Masada before them—
that there was no other way.
They drew straws.

The first Spaniard to awaken
was startled by the hush, as though
the earth itself had given up.
He stepped out into the chill,
into the stained silence,
but saw only flowers, thousands
of flamboyáns—

splashes of blood—

blooming all over the island.

Taínos—*native inhabitants of Boriquén (Taíno name for Puerto Rico), an
agrarian peaceful tribe of potters and weavers. Many who were not deci-
mated by the Spanish colonists committed suicide en masse.*

Guanín—*gold medallion worn by the chief of the Taínos.*

Anita Vélez-Mitchell

TÓTEM TAÍNO

El Taíno vivía en las Cumbres
La paz era su nobleza
de su enemigo el Caribe
se refugiaba en las cuevas
su defensa arco y flecha

Cuando infieles avarientos
desembarcan en sus playas
con su complejo de altura
perros y armas de fuego
dispuestos a la batalla

Les arrebatan sus cumbres
le profanan su culto,
su cueva, roban su oro,
raptan sus mujeres bellas,
esclavizan sus hijos,
rompen su arco y su flecha

Muere el Cacique Agüeybaná,
el valeroso guerrero
su piel tatuada en colores
su guanín de oro al cuello

Colgado de un flamboyán
su alma al cielo ascendió
su grito encaracolao se ahogó
en la cueva de su corazón

Hoy su alma aún nos clama
emplumada en la conciencia
y nos gime y lagrimea
del interior de sus cuevas
la madre naturaleza

Ya el tiempo ha madurado
los corazones de piedra
prueba el dulzor de sus frutos

y de las flores su esencia
la virtud de su inocencia

Quiera Diós no se repita
la presencia del malvado
y el dolor de ser esclavo
dentro de su propia tierra

Y los mares se huracanan
Y de Boriquén emana
un areyto al corazón
cual un volcán en el pecho,
lava de la inspiración

Taíno de Amor y Paz
Boriquén es tu nación
te imploramos ¡Ay, bendito Diós!
Una mina de perdón....

Perdón ... perdón ... perdón.

TÓTEM TAÍNO

Inspired by the Caves of Camuy, Puerto Rico

The Taíno lived on the mountain,
peace was his noble bequest,
to evade his enemy, the Caribe,
he took refuge in the caves,
a bow and arrow his sole defense

When the avaricious infidels
disembark on his shore—
with their smugness and swagger,
their dogs and firearms ready for war—
they plunder his mountains,

profane his culture, his caves,
rape his women, enslaved
his children, steal his gold,
and shatter his arc and his bow.

They seize Cacique Agüeybaná,
their leader, intrepid and bold,
his skin tattooed in colors,
on his chest a medallion of gold

and hang him from a flamboyán tree
His soul ascends to heaven,
but his cry remains entombed
in the heart of his hollow cave,
locked in our conscience forever
where his spirit still claims us today.
Sobs reverberate, thick tears drop
in the cavernous womb of mother earth.

Time has softened our pride
and melted our hearts of stone.

In the sweetness of our fruits,
the essence of our flowers
and the beauty of our land,

the Taíno soul lives on.

Let us pray those evil intruders
never dare return
to destroy a nation and enslave a people
on their own soil, as they did back then.

Let the oceans rage and rise,
let the lava from Boriquén flow,
let it cleanse our guilt
and guide us back to the *areyto*,
back to the ritual chant of the Taíno.

Taíno of love and peace,
Boriquén is your homeland—
we offer you, blesséd spirits,
a goldmine of regret.
We implore you—*¡Ay bendito Diós!*—

forgive us...forgive us...forgive us.

Taíno: *the indigenous people of Puerto Rico*
Areyto: *the ritual chant of the Taíno*
Boriquén: *the Taíno name for Puerto Rico*
guanín: *medallion*
flamboyán: *a tall red flowering tree*
¡Ay bendito Diós!: *literally, Oh, blesséd God, a common
    Puerto Rican interjection*

MIRAMAR, Puerto Rico

Through a window of an exclusive
ocean-view apartment in Miramar,
we witness a hold-up.

"Hurry! *Vengan!* Over there!"
Nanny calls to us, pointing.

A woman flutters up the sloping street,
flustered, arms winging, purseless.

A man flees. Who is he?
"Ni la sombra." Nanny says.
Just a shadow. She runs to
check the iron gates.

All we can do is gasp. My cousin
crosses herself. In the background
the palm trees fan the sultry air.

It is noon. The church bells chime.

The sun drops its light on
our anxious faces. Silent,
we finish lunch, then break into
the pointless issue of drugs,

the problem of the problem.

The shameless assault on the cooing birds,
the muffled scream that shooed them away.

The wind rattles the shutters.
Nanny utters: *"Esto
no se lo lleva el viento."* No,
this will never blow away.

My cousin prays.
We nod, resigned to being truly captive.
We hear the seagulls cry.
The palm trees sway.

BIRTHRIGHT

My daughter sat naked on these tiles,
a two-year old side-stepping
diapers and safety pins, out-running
my father and me across the stone

mandalas set rim to rim from one
end of this open house to the other.
I trace the pattern now with my bare toe,
a gingerly caress growing cold

as a lawyer demands to see my birth
certificate—as if my lineage were
in question here. My father's widow
grieves in spurts, afraid she'll lose

her house to me. Tomorrow
I shall leave this place behind; leave
the coldness of tiles and skin and words,
leave my inheritance—a small space

in a corner of my father's world—
and my identity, for what it's worth.

Anika Paris

ON BUYING OUR FIRST HOUSE MOMENTS BEFORE THE MORTGAGE CRISIS

I proudly nudge our Obama/Biden sign
into the soil of our front lawn
pairing it shoulder to shoulder with
that little Maple tree
struggling to survive California's summer heat.

We got in under the wire with a "no doc" loan
from Fanny Mae, our new friend.
We're almost middle aged, officially middle class,
      according to my dad,
who boasted it loud enough for all the neighbors to hear.
We bought a white picket fence and the American dream.

For eleven years we resided in a rental held together
with glue and endured a no-fix-it landlord.
Still we kept "soupin' up the Pinto,"
moving the couch from one wall to another
as if that would change our perception.

We could see each other from every non-air-conditioned room
and I, inevitably morphing into my mother, kept
our morale alive by remembering the less fortunate
living in mud huts, sleeping on cardboard boxes,
limbless, with no food, no hope.

Today I call out to Dean with amusement:
I can't find him *anywhere* in our new house.
We've named her Little Buckingham—
buttermilk curtains and open-armed windows
overlooking a lavender hill.

On the back patio under latticed bougainvillea
I decide to paint a still life to capture the moment.
I fetch the newspaper to protect the veneer, unfolding our future
page by page: warnings of economic hemorrhaging,
bankroll bleed-outs, mortgage meltdowns.

32

I make fresh-squeezed orange juice,
grind the rind to my "I've got a disposal" dance,
rumba for the icemaker,
tango while summoning the plates and cutlery
to attention in the dishwasher, do the laundry Lambada,

blast the AC, and Tivo my favorite shows.
I'm dancing with the stars.

NUYORICAN LAMENT

San Juan you're not for me.
My cadence quails and stumbles
on your ancient stones:

there is an inner beat here
to be reckoned with—
a *seis chorreao*, a *plena*,
an inbred *¡Oyeeee!*
and *¡mira tú!* against which
my Manhattan (sorry
wrong island) responses fall flat.

¡Vaya! How can I deal with that?

And yet. . . once, long ago,
your beach was mine; Luquillo
was my bridle path to ride—
back then, before the turning of the tide
when Teddy's blue-eyed shills
secured the hill
and tried in vain to blot
the language out. But *patria*

is a sneaky word—it lies,
seeming to turn its back
upon itself—it lies,
through paling generations—lies
        and lies in wait:
the sleeping dog of nations
no translation can obliterate

(and when it's roused—
beware the bully
beware the apple pie).

I rode with purpose then,
back then, when
you were mine, harnessing

the strength of iron
in my thighs—
my eyes blazing with self, my self
with pride—

and once, at La Parguera,
I was baptized
on a moonless night in spring,
emerging purged and
reinvented, the phosphorescent
spangles clinging
to my skin, signaling
the night to bless my innocence—

then, only yesterday—or so it seems—
I spent my youth
in La Princesa's dungeon
for unproved crimes
against an unloved nation—yes

only yesterday, I knew where I belonged,
I knew my part.

And now, you see me here,
a trespasser in my own past,
tracing a faint ancestral theme
far back, beyond the hard rock
rhythm of the strand.
I walk down El Condado, past
Pizza Huts, Big Macs and
Coca-cola stands
listening for a song—

a wisp of song—

that begs deep in my heart.

La Princesa: *The jail.*

Anita Vélez-Mitchell

JAZZ

—Homage to Luigi

It's a cool grey morning.
I walk in haste up 57th Street
towards Central Park
to my daily jazz class with Luigi.

I pass an old Carusophile
across from the Art Students League,
who, with cross and hat in hand,
insists on croaking aria after aria
in a continual plea for change.

Luigi's witticism comes to mind:

Do it over and over,
again and again, but brother,
unless you do it right,
you'll do it perfectly
wrong forever.

A seeing-eye dog leads
a blind man across
Columbus Circle. He's in danger.
I rush to see him through.
Luigi's maxim calls for action:

Never stop moving,
never stop moving.

I walk hurriedly on, see
a teenaged hooker lounging by
the fountain at Gulf & Western.
The brief encounter with
flashes of reality invades my senses,
slows my tempo down. Once more
I hear Luigi's voice resound:

Don't look around.

Feel your own essence.
No two people are alike.
Listen to the rhythms
of your own making.

Almost running now,
anxious to get to where
I tear off my clothes and
dress down for a workout
that synthesizes body and soul,
rises to a freedom one attains
through the energized expression
of self, in time and space—

and there is Luigi, a clarion call to art,
who will zazz up your cells
with the fugit art of dance—
the sound, the step, the beat,
where even sweat smells sweet.

You can do it—listen to the music
and you'll become the music.
Once more, again,
four, five, six, seven, eight, turn.

Now, his famous walk to fame....
Learn we must. Yes, we finally do it
and bow. The focus off, then,
soulfully, Luigi breathes in
our applause.

LEAP FROG

My mother, a fair-skinned Puerto Rican told me
she married my father hoping to have exotic children
Her sister Jane told me she always felt like the dark one
I, blonde and blue-eyed, only wanted Jordache jeans
and unlike my older sister, shaved my legs
without my mother's permission to fit in
at the all-girl private school I attended

We third-generationers get the watered down
version of our grandparents' stories
the language barrier widening in time
the evolution of technology carrying us into the future
while the coquí's song fades in the distance

Even though my Spanish is unlearned
my ears understand it
my hips and feet talk back when the Taínos play

I grew up on the beach in Texas with
tropical palm trees and a yellow sun escorting me
most of my young life, and I've returned to it
buying a little house in California with honeysuckle-
flavored air, longing to run barefoot across the moist grass
and pick loquats from the arms of trees
And still the coquí's song fades in the distance

It only sings in Puerto Rico
where it feels at home
I want to go back to where I've never been
and sing along

BICOASTAL:
THE SELL DATE ON MY LIFE HAS EXPIRED

I dream I'm in New York City,
wake up in California, walk
into the wall. I turn right to
go to the bathroom, walk into
a closet. I'm out of toilet
paper, even though I bought 12
rolls at Costco 5 days ago.
I turn on the cold water, scald
myself. It's five a.m. I'm out
of milk, the eggs are three months old.
Vital files have vanished from my
computer. I hear it dial unfamiliar
staccato notes. No DSL.
The signed Karl Shapiro on my
night stand is by V.S. Naipaul.
The clothes in my closet are two
sizes too small, my favorite
jacket is gone. Where are my shoes?
I'm afraid to drive the car—it's
a hybrid. I drive north, wind up
in Baja with strangers, who look
familiar. Back home, my husband
storms into the living room. "Can't
find my watch, can't find my wallet!"
Mere trifle. I can't find my*self*!

FREEDOM IN CENTRAL PARK

(Written in the 1930s in Spanish)

I'm free...alone with myself
in this green span of leisure
I speak to the pigeons
and they teach me how
to look for food

The wind urges me on,
wants to help me
escape from myself
from my inaccessible dreams
my desires, my longings.
Ah, to be back with those
at home on the island
of Vieques, my abused
green homeland I love!

Gone. Gone forever.

I lie on the grass
the colors change to blue
and those dreams, those desires
bring tears to my eyes.

It's late, I guess, as legs hurry by.
I see a shadow—a colorful skirt
above me. I must get up
from the chitty-chat of green.
The wind lifts me.
I must return to the fold.

Somehow, like my beloved island,
it too has been torn apart:
the arguments, the scolding,
the nasty talk, secrets and
stories not told to me.
Shh, loud as bombs, and
She's only a child, they say.

40

With an effort I push the wind
from my face and look far away.
I take a deep breath and say
good-bye to the earth, to the sky.
The setting sun cradles my shadow,
but the space overwhelms me.

Central Park is immense
like my aunt's arms extended
in a tearful goodbye.

Is it south, east, west, north?
The wind insists *go on...go home.*
with a frown of concern I tell my feet
to *go on*...but where? *Where?*

Where is home?

BORDER LINE

Puerto Nuevo or New Port in English
is 40 miles from the border of Mexico
It's Saturday and there's a slight
overcast on our venture

¿Quieren comida? they say, courting us
with brown sugar smiles and honey-glazed eyes
Men like paparazzi perched outside their restaurants
begging to cook us a meal
pleading to serve us anything
as we glitter their muddy streets

The salty air hangs heavy
on my conscience
on the roof of this restaurant
on the rim of my margarita
bittersweetly blended in chartreuse

We sit overlooking the village
and sing out to the mariachi band below:
"La cucaracha, la cucaracha, ya no puede caminar"
till all twelve trot up the stairs
playing guitars, horns, drums and violins
bursting at the seams of indigo blue
wearing shiny sombreros and sequined desperation
I trace the sound with the tips of my fingers
and lose myself for a moment

Yet, on the brim of our echo
I can't help noticing across the street
a woman on the roof of a tenement
that's burnt to a seaweed crisp
its coffee-stained sheets unable to hide
the naked rooms inside
This building sagging slightly to the left
barely held together with wire hangers
pouts over the junked cars
climbing its doorway like spiders

And amidst all this American novelty
and façade of celebration
the woman washes her family's clothes
scrubs each shirt, each pair of pants
each mud-stained sock
unable to rinse out their future

"*Se sirve el almuerzo,*
langosta deliciosa para todas
las señoritas hermosas," the owner says
unfolding a blanket of food
his wife and children catering to us like royalty
filling our cups till they overflow
basting our plates with homemade salsa
succulent lobster in melted butter
rice, beans, and warm corn tortillas
individually wrapped

The mariachi band is still playing
my friends are laughing and clapping in rhythm
dancing on the rooftop
even the sun decides to finally visit

But I can't eat

LANDLOCKED IN KANSAS

I don't know about harvests and corn,
about hornworms or tomato blights.
Saw my first cow at seventeen,
though I was on a first-name basis
with an elephant at Ringling's,
let him lift me to the heavens
in his tuba-furled trunk—a bond
neither of us ever forgot. Delicious
that ride above heads, my mother urging
"be brave, be brave," not knowing
my delirium, my love of heights and
speed and danger was defining itself
there, then, stretching through the next
twenty-odd years when I would
search out possibilities of near-death
the way others sought favor, riches,
with a kind of steadfast abandon
and denial of rules and gravity.
I rose higher than an elephant's eye,
but not an ear of corn in sight—my
fields, sand-lot diamonds; my lanes,
congested streets crisscrossing the city,
streetlights casting eerie circles of
diminishing returns across the pavement
below, squares of concrete, greedy
for light, guzzling every drop, every
neon drop. I lied about the sandlots,
a good image, but not *my* lot—suburban
brown was out of my spectrum; life
for me was black and white and I, though
always on the wrong side—Latina and
fair, was often on the right, as well:
Up in the stratosphere, ready to leap, fly,
tumble, fall free; eager for the next break,
the next thrill, the final escape.

KITCHEN KARMA

I redecorated the entire house
for our New Year's Eve party
squeegee'd every window pane
on our French doors, swept
behind the couch, dusted the molding
around the den on my hands and knees
shined the chandelier or
whatever you want to call it
color coded the coat closet
bought new wooden hangers
pulled out our crystal champagne flutes
arranged a bouquet of exotic flowers
from Pierre's on the Plaza
in the Lalique vase your mother bought us
hired Katie's catering service and
her famous cheese soufflé
booked a new Sarah Vaughan trio
sent out custom-designed invitations on
mint green rice paper to
65 *powerhouse, soon to be, up and coming,*
has beens, and *wannabes* to our party.

So somebody please tell me
what the hell is everyone doing in the kitchen?

Mothers and Daughters

CHORUS LINE

My mother's photo is missing
from my amulet, just as mine
is missing from her piano. My
daughter laughs each time she visits,
searches for her face among the
8x10s lined up like beauties
in a contest—nope, didn't make
the cut this week. Who among us,
she wonders, has done something
grand enough to be included in
the dance of fame? Her aunt?
Her sister? Her brother? Or is it
someone my mother met at a party—
a new face to brag about—or
the singer she felt sorry for, who
entertains passengers in the subway?
The rest of us come and go.
Stars one week, has-beens the next—
shades of Off-Broadway. The only
constant on the piano lid is Mother,
who leads us in this crazy dance.

Anita Vélez-Mitchell

THE MILKY WAY

I am in empathy
with the Kansas sky.
Ghost clusters of clouds
bring back my childhood
when I'd stretch out
on the welcoming grass
and see, deep into space,
my absent mother.

Here she is again
moving tenderly across
my aching heart.
Her florid skirt
turning from white to
deep purple as she hides
then reappears
as if pulled back and
forth by a sacred hand.

Mamí, I cry out
into this ghost-loved world
but there is no echo
to my call from afar.
Like a glow swathed
in dust set to keep us
apart, my mother's ghost
fades away to make
way for a star.

SYNTHESIS

for Gloria and Bill

Climb the spiral staircase
to the playground I built for you in heaven
where I laid down a magic carpet of artificial grass
planted Cacti in boxes
and collected just enough lawn chairs
so we can see beyond the power poles
twisted wires and polluted air

I built it while you were away
Now we'll talk at sunset
without being blinded by the western glare
turn our backs on the ominous ocean
a few minutes a day
watching the birds fly overhead
here in our make believe world
two stories closer to God

Perhaps we'll even fall in love
all over again

ISLANDS: ISLA MADRE, ISLA NENA

"I'm convinced the ocean is a conveyor, not an isolator."
—Thor Heyerdahl

My mother stands at the water's edge
on the barrier island of Vieques.
She waits for her mother to come to her.
Sunday after Sunday she waits,
the water stretching to that other
shore in the impossible geography
of her extended heart.

As a child I too waited
for my mother to come.
Sunday after Sunday, behind
the wrought iron fence that
quarantined the schoolyard, I waited—
the whiteness of a car, any car,
revving my heart's sappy rhythm.

And still we wait, we two, still,
so still, each on our own atoll, each
in our own sorrow, though I suspect
the ocean could drown the land
and take my mother to her mother
by the hand, leaving me bereft.

RADIO

In boarding school we were given a choice:
Sinatra on "The Hit Parade" or Gene Autry,
and being an urban kid I'd always opt for
Autry, the Singing Cowboy, as different
as anyone could ever be from anyone
I'd ever known—but the older girls chose
Frankie and so *he* crooned us to sleep
on Saturday nights. When I turned eleven
I went to live with my mother and new
stepfather, a humorless man, who'd send me
to my room each time I'd giggle.
"*Está en la edad del pavo*, she's in
the turkey age," Abuelita would explain,
not realizing I loved being exiled
to my own radio and my own choices,
where I could listen undisturbed to
"Inner Sanctum," with its creaking door;
"The Fat Man," weighing in at 250 pounds,
his fortune, *Danger*; "The Green Hornet,"
buzzing around with his sidekick Kato;
or my favorite, "The Shadow." *He* knew
no evil lurked in my young heart, even
though I had to be sent away to school!
He knew I meant no harm when I would
torment my grandmother with cries
of *tighter! tighter!*, until both shoelaces
were equally taut, both braids equally
tight, my hair parted in the exact center.
Those mornings must have been trying
for her, before she would walk me
to kindergarten and sigh with relief
as my little hand let go of hers. But I
paid dearly for my so-called sins:
a long stint in the hinterlands of love.
And only The Shadow, my invisible ally,
could corroborate my innocence.

A MI MADRE, LUCILA RIECKEHOFF

Luz...Luz...Luz...

¡Qué larga la ausencia
oceánica
de tu imantado ser!
¡Qué inmenso paisaje
de distancia!

Yo,
diminuta,
perdida,
te buscaba
en los coloquios curvados
del mar.
Hasta en el corazón
de mi inocencia
creía encontrarte.

¿Cómo me ibas a dejar
sin tí?
¡Qué larga la niñez
sin tu presencia!
Parecía una eternidad,
un manantial de ternura
ahogado en el pozo
de mi soledad.

Al fin llegastes...madre,
un día sin fiesta,
con la niña de tus ojos rota.
Te parecías a mí
y yo a tí.
Dolor de dos ausencias.
El corazón habitado
por pájaros ciegos
no nos permitía vernos.
Había entrado ya

la avestruz de la indiferencia
en el nido sagrado del amor.

"Ya no soy tu nena, mamá,"
gritó mi dolor.
Luz...Luz...Luz...
De tanta oscuridad
la luz nos ciega.

Anita Vélez-Mitchell

TO MY MOTHER, LUCILA RIECKEHOFF

Luz...Luz...Luz...

How vast the oceanic
absence
of your magnetic image!
How immense the distance
of your journey!

I,
tiny,
lost,
searched for you
in the curved conversation
of the sea.
I even thought
I would find you
in the core of my innocence.

How could you possibly
leave me?
My childhood was endless
without your presence!
It seemed an eternity—
a spring of tenderness
drowned in the well
of my solitude.

At last you came, Mother,
an ordinary day,
the pupils of your eyes
distressed.
We looked alike, we two:
each wearing the pain
of absence. Sightless
birds locked in my heart
obscured my vision.

Indifference
had already invaded
love's sacred nest.

"I'm no longer your child, Mamá,"
screamed my pain.
Luz...Luz...Luz...
After so much darkness,
light blinds us.

Luz: *Light; and also a shortened form of the name Lucila*

REFLECTION

In the elevator mirror, I see her, still
disapproving. One eyebrow raised just so.

She examines me, curiously, almost
as if she were hoping to catch something

out of whack. I stare back, defiant. Shocked
to see how old she's gotten in so short

a time, how she's assumed that crusty stare.
I smile, adjust my lipstick, see her smile—

big, lamia-mouth, ready to devour me.
Oh, Mother, I say to her face—I, who

have never said one contradictory
word to her—not a *no*, not a *but*—say

to her now: *Let me go!* But the words sound
suspiciously like, *Love me! Please love me!*

POETIC PLAYGROUND

(or dodgeball and tetherations)

Miss Ramon
should have been a dead giveaway
she was single in the '70s
in Corpus Christi, Texas
an elementary school teacher and Jesus freak

Our assignment: alliterations
Mine turned into a Wrath from God
I was only eight
I didn't know what the word "rape" even meant
I must have heard it at Nancy's house
I was focusing on the *r*'s in Ramon and Rodney
who sat next to me
with a blonde Beatles haircut
and troubled soul

But I did it *this* time
Rude Rodney Raped Miss Ramon
I blurted out proudly when called upon
in class, rolling the *r*'s
with a Latin flair like my mother does
sharing my new-found lyricism
a poet with wings
standing tall on my bucket of sin

I felt the fiery stares and silence
walked the halls of shame
to the principal's office
my stomach twisted in a fist of confusion
everything in s l o w   m o t i o n

My mother pleaded my case
"What's wrong, it's a perfectly good alliteration!"
her laughter spinning like the tetherball
I later hit in Menger's playground

Anika Paris

above everyone's head
in both directions
rewriting eighteen new alliterations
with every swing
Rude Rodney Raided Miss Ramon's Refrigerator
Rude Rodney Ransacked Rudy's Restaurant
Rude Rodney got paddled
Well, he actually did
while I, held together by a string of paperclips
waited to be shipped off into outer space
cast out and expelled
Mom found it very humorous
and I dodged hell

INSIGHT

She is beautiful—even now at 89,
when she retells the story, the retelling
more telling each time; each time
the child is older, fears more for the child
within the child grown up.

She is beautiful—even now at 91, recounting
to the child, now grown, what happened
on that strange day, the day she met the Spaniard.
Sonja introduced them at a nightclub.
("Who is Sonja?" "She was my friend.")

They had been talking about dance,
elevation in ballet where the dancer praises
the sky: *la lluvia*—the rain—for nourishing
the crops, giving them beauty and strength,
el sol—the sun—for preserving life.

"I could never dance flamenco," she says,
"it is a dance of resentment and anger, heels
tapatiando—pounding—the unyielding land."
"So young, so beautiful, and so wrong,"
the Spaniard says. "If you believe that, you
do not know the dance." He offers to take her
to Carnegie Hall the following night
to see the great La Argentinita perform.

He picks her up at her apartment, way up
in Spanish Harlem. They did that in those days,
pick you up. Her little girl opens the door.
He lifts her up to get a better look.
Her eyes seem fixated on some secret memory.
One does not move; but *he* is moved.

We're talking here of a beautiful single mother

of a cross-eyed 5-year-old and of a world-famous
ophthalmologist, who has come from Spain
to open an eye clinic in the United States.
What are the odds of that happening?
"Bring her to the hospital tomorrow at nine."
He writes down the address, and they leave.

The next morning she brings him her child.
"Come back in three hours." He gives her
money to take in a movie. She protests, of course.
How can she leave her child? "She'll play with
the other children," he explains, And she agrees.

What movie did she see? Or did she use
the money to buy food for the family?
She can't remember. When she returns,
her daughter has a bandage over her left eye.
"She'll be fine," he says. "Bring her back in a week."
And she so young, so naive, so beautiful—
though, she insists, he never even tried to kiss her.

He cares for the child at his clinic on
Manhattan's upper East Side, cares for her
until the child marries and moves away, her eyes
as straight and beautiful as her mother's.
Had his name not been Ramon Castroviejo,
she would have named her first daughter after him.

The child, now the mother of a five-year-old, gasps
on hearing her mother retell the story.
"I can't believe you sold me for the price of a movie!"
Then, quickly, "But I'm so glad you did!"
And her mother? She became a flamenco dancer.

EMPTY NESTER

The bicycle becomes an issue
hanging upside down
in the garage.
Out of the way, really,
his wife insists,
but it triggers his anger,
his sense of loss.
Get rid of it, he says,
takes up too much room.
When the movers come
he doesn't tell her until
it's too late. She sees
the shiny blue chrome
the color of her daughter's eyes
lying in the truck bed
like a casualty.

SYMBOL OF A DREAM

Jane's posture
was still visible
in the clothes
she left behind,
though they were
neatly hung.

Folding her
outgrown shirts
I was reminded
of a snake
shedding its skin.

That night I dreamt
I was trying on
her shirt.
The buttons
fell off
and scattered
all over the floor
changing into
flowery pompoms.

As I anxiously
scurried after them
I woke up, disturbed,
and analyzed
my dream.
Jane's shirts and buttons
parted....
The flower falls off
when the fruit is born.

She's ambitious, grown,
and gone.

But shirts and buttons
go together
as a dream
needs a dreamer.

This is Jane's home.

Anita Vélez-Mitchell

BREAKING THE SILENCE (OR WHY I SOL[THE SKY, THE SEA, THE LILACS, AND AND THE HOUSE THAT BOUND THEM)

To my daughter Jane

Then one day
your dad knew his days
were counted

He sat silently,
as before a fire, sat
on the porch facing
the lilacs and the ocean
and the sky, while

I, bluer than sky or sea,
and misty as the lilacs,
cried and cried

It could have been
a song to his guitar
we would all end up
singing, but we both
felt as if it had already
happened

He knew he was dying,
wanted to be alone
with his thoughts
before parting and

I, remaining behind
closed doors, listened
to his utter silence

A few days later
he was gone
The house by the sea
became a tomb—

memories of him and
me and you, our child—
a closed album of
the past I could no longer
open without weeping

It could have been a song
to his guitar, when we
would all join in—
friends, neighbors, family—
on Sunday afternoons

But now it was the blues—
that ocean, that sky,
and those misty lilacs
he loved—gone
with his infinite silence

Anika Paris

BABY DEPOT

I'm sitting next to 40
and still thinking I want a baby
then I quickly change my mind
I have no money and no room in my house
I'm not even married
and I think I'm in college

My father told me to just get pregnant
paint every room pink
and not to worry about it

Maybe I'll take his advice
and go to Home Depot
pick out a color swatch
buy an ovulation kit, while I'm at it
and jump start my love life again

Am I suppose to time it, as my sister-in-law did
lie with my legs in the air
and hope for a crash landing?

I wonder if my landlord
appropriately named Mr. Ohno
would let us build an addition off the kitchen
next to the washer and dryer
where junior could sleep
to the whooshing and swooshing sounds
of the delicate cycle

Good call on the pink paint I guess
a wise old man my father is
but wait a second—
what if it's a boy?

SNOWED IN
—for Paul

On the slopes I'm out of control
falling is hard, not falling, harder.
I turn my back on soaring, turn my back
on challenges and leaving my snow-
laden son to face the elements alone
trace my way home to a paned
panorama of frenzy and grace.

I can cope with that.

Sipping mulled tea I watch
the evergreens and aspens welcome
winter, hear their icy branches
insistent at my window, trying to tell me
what I already know. I can still
make out each separate bough, see
it gently shrugging off the years.
Tomorrow these trees will look regal,
their spines upright and strong, and
before long they'll be making green
and gracious overtures to spring.

I dread the snow, hide from it, knowing
that each flake will leave its mark.

In the distance everything is out
of focus. I see through my son's
myopic eyes the hazy landscape as he
braves the coming storm.

KEEP IN TOUCH

To my daughter Gloria

The touch of your palm
leaves your heart in mine
as we walk together.
The weather is spring-like,
the ambience, a delight!
What has your hand got
that brings me joy?
Must be love, touching love
through our fingertips, playfully
rushing to our brain,
brightening our eyes.
Or...is it the hidden angst
of being away from each other
for such a long time,
bubbling over so many absences,
and now bursting with pride—
the two of us together
walking side by side.

MY HANDS GREET EACH OTHER
AS IF FOR THE FIRST TIME

The day begins early: doctor's visit, post-op.
Last thing I remember before going under
is doctor's hand holding mine—a warm,
fleshy, casual hold. I thank her. She smiles.
Back home, my computer crashes
with my life. I weep. Wring my hands.
Call all the nerds I know. And wait
till they call back. Just as I am about
to give up, one calls to say he will come
that evening. I am saved. I wipe
my tears, rush to accept the last-minute
invitation I refused an hour earlier.
As I am about to leave, a special delivery
arrives—a redwhiteandblue banner
covered with has-been stamps from ten,
twenty, thirty years ago, stamps of faces,
landmarks, events, frozen in time, frozen
in a kind of forced delirium—forced or not,
the sparks leap to my heart and I laugh
at the utter clutter of colors, shapes, sizes—
boisterous and frisky—ready to spring
from the package and cover my face with
kisses. I carry the gift with me to lunch,
unopened like a secret love letter, wanting
to share its madness with friends. We giggle
at its garishness. Giggle at its contents:
a T-shirt about shame and its consequences.
and curled within the shirt, an immense
white silk scarf patterned with my logo,
black helixes. And within that, a note
from my mother—bearer of good tidings,
good timing—to wear it with joy.
I wear the scarf to dinner and sit
smiling sappily at the thought of stamps—
68 of them!—stampeding to my door.
I clasp my hands in sheer delight and find
to my astonishment that I am
holding my mother's hand in mine.

THE MOUSE THAT ROARED

(Erasmo Vando 1898-1991)

My father was a little man
with a big voice, a voice so loud
he could assemble a crowd
around him in one instant:
¡Oigan, amigos!, he would bellow from

his soapbox and they would listen—
leaning out of windows, gathering
on stoops, packed around him
eager to catch his every word.
He was a New World troubadour

bringing the bad news
to Puerto Rican Harlem:
"Uncle Sam has stolen our land,"
he'd shout. "It's time we stand
up to him and demand it back!"

"*¡Si, hombre, si!*" they'd shout
in response. "You tell 'em, Vando!"
And one Monday he did,
addressing the U.N., that swell
body of big powerful men

with soft voices, who listened
intently to my little father,
but heard nothing, saw nothing,
did nothing—no matter how loud
and how long he yelled.

MAURICE'S RETURN

For my father, China, December 2003

It's been awhile since I've seen my father conduct—
and China, of all places.
Mozart's 29th, Bernstein's Three Meditations,
and Prokofiev are the guests of honor.

The concert hall is cold and dim,
amenities scarce.
Hard wooden chairs with their mouths open
wait and stare.

Little by little tiny bodies
and a sea of dark hair, with
voices marbling about, fill the room
until the first violinist appears.

Maurice, Dad to me,
Maestro, to the rest of the world,
glides onstage
a chest full of fire,
arms outstretched—a lion—
he takes to the podium.

With one stroke of the baton
he paints the air with Mozart's melodies
swelling up in waves
pirouetting towards heaven
and back down again.

Flutes and violins
tickling the nape of my neck,
trombones, tubas, and timpanis
rumbling in meditations,
shaking the floorboards beneath us
until a cello's cry bends the night
into a lullaby.

Black dots on paper,

120 players, a man with a stick,
wood, brass, and hammers
create this intangible beauty,
blurring the lines that define us,
stirring up the mercury of this damp country,
turning it red, like its flag—
a circle of fire, vibrant and alive—
with sounds of forbidden love affairs.

I sit row eight, dead center,
and listen with a new perspective.
Listen in awe,
watching my father
and the gift he brings.

He is soaring,
he's in love,
He is home.

Gloria Vando

MY 90-YEAR-OLD FATHER AND MY HUSBAND
DISCUSS THEIR TRIPS TO THE MOON
–for Bill

On the balcony I hear my father
speak of craters, their depth, their breadth;
how he measured his lunar steps so as not to falter,

sidestepping their cavernous mouths to peer in,
his echo resounding in their hearts.
He was on the moon's good side, the one

that smiles and on occasion winks at the earth.
With audible pride, he explains he was the lone
civilian on the mission. Yet he was happy to come home.

Yes, my husband says, *it was wonderful for me, too!*
Shepard led me by the hand around the rim
of Eratosthenes. My father laughs at the similarity

of the crater's name to his own, Erasmus.
He is glad Bill understands him,
relieved someone else knows how desolate it can be

out there. *Not only desolate*, Bill says,
putting an arm around my father's frail shoulders,
I also know how lonely it can get.

SHE SITS ON MY HUSBAND'S LAP

attacks the space around her, punching
here, slapping there, her fist slamming
into the butter on the table, knocking over
the milk pitcher, all the while moaning
an inarticulate wail, low and hollow,
as if a wind storm loose in her body were
blasting out through all the broken spaces
she cannot keep together. He holds her
to him, strokes her matted hair, rocks and
rocks her little body until the fury subsides.

I watch Mariana, her six-year-old frame
curled and shivering intermittently the way
our bodies do after we've cried a lot.
Her mother, Emelí, smiles at me. "She'll
sleep for awhile now. It's always like that."
I want to ask her how she can stand it day after
day. Does she ever wish she'd not been born?
Her smile answers what I cannot fathom.

"Try some *turrón*," she says, offering
us pieces of almond nougat candy.
She pours a glass of Madeira, the tawny color
of Mariana's hair, and passes it to me.
Bill eats with one hand, carefully picks
up a crumb floating on Mariana's cheek.
While she sleeps, her body heavy and hot,
her pale blue dress damp and twisted
against his chest, we talk of other things.

Tomorrow we will go to Cerro Maravilla,
the most beautiful peak in the mountain.
From there you can see the entire island.
"The legend goes," Emelí says, "that if you
concentrate you can see heaven." We laugh.
"I thought *this* might be heaven," Bill says.
"Maybe it's the last step on the ladder."

–for Bill, remembering our first trip to Puerto Rico

THE KING

He tucks his mane beneath a silent roar
meek and aged
reverence scorned by a feline fury
out on the hunt for his throne

They care not, want not
to know of his imminent battle
and dance along the trails
he paved for them

His eyes are pinched
shoulders curled
arms punching the air
warding off the demons and darkness
with a crumpled fist

Fear not this feeble king
as he gasps for breath
no longer majestic
only skin and bones
wearing a crown too big for his head.

DANCING MAN

For Pearse

When this man dies,
forget those little stars.
      They were okay in Shakespeare's day
      when candles couldn't hold their own
      against the evening sky;
today, the sentiment's passé.
Gaudy neon—not the sun—is king.

If he must go—up or out or wherever
whatever we become must go—
      let it be one mighty act:
A supernova of such magnitude and breadth
that it renews itself at will,
blazing through eternity, illuming
universes, mooning earth (evil
mother of decay and fear), defying death.

I have seen my dad (in deed
      not blood) gear down.
I have felt his dull flesh, loose against its bony
frame, turn cool and smooth as plasticene
      thirsting for light.
He lies in bed, his limbs unclaimed, feet
      distended, as though spiting
him with pent-up rhapsodies
      of dancing nights.

Astaire, they called him then, a young Astaire,
matching his body's rhythm in easy elegance
      to the dance,
claiming the title, holding on forever—
      what a tinsel word, forever!
Now only the cane remains steadfast,
helping him past the obstacle of pain.
      The top hat's shelved,
      the shoes have danced their last.
The light within is dimming fast, so fast.

And in the other room, my mother,
growing strong as he declines,
whispers of summer when they plan
to dine and dance the nights away,
          contemplates a face lift the day
he is consigned to bed.
My mother, an aging movie queen?
A centerfold? A widow on the make?
No, just plain scared. "You know,"
she says, "I've never danced alone."

One night while he's asleep
we sneak out for a spell
to the Parker Meridien, a new hotel
          across the street, where
          a woman at the keyboard sings
their songs. Songs of disappointment,
longing, clinging to the skin of memory
like the noxious smell of illness
we are desperate to dispel. Small comfort
          in the welling loneliness
          of nights to come.

"No sad songs for me," he used to say.
          No minor keys.
          Yet only he knew
every word of every verse and every chorus,
only he could turn each song into a tragic story.
          "Irish to the core," she'd say.

And as he sleeps, we sit across the street,
eating nuts and pretzels, sipping wine,
listening to the mournful sounds
          of "Funny Valentine,"
          and weep.
For I'm to be abandoned yet again
when this kind man, who let me in
          and gave me dance,
          is gone.

THE BIGGER PICTURE

A sense of sadness is hanging around
no matter what I try to do
the world goes on in spite of my life
How is this possible?
Don't they know who I am?

Today's headline, *Michael Jackson Dead*
will disappear from every global paper
and become a history lesson
his songs and stories a terabyte of information
inevitably to be lost in an Ice Age of cyberspace.
Or that xeroxed black and white copy
of my grandmother's family portrait
that we show every Passover
naming each one killed in the Holocaust
will be forgotten with each generation.
Even the nameless headstone
in Potter's Field someone left flowers on
will sink into the earth with time.

And suddenly I feel so mortal
at the edge of the ocean
so disposable and unimportant
in the bigger picture.
I'm reminded I'm just a microscopic piece
in this endlessness every time I fly
and look out my window
searching for my house in the speckles of earth
seeing how small we really are
and realize each one holds a story
and that it all can go on
will go on
when I'm gone.

We all know we'll end.
Some find God
some check out
some get whisked away in the wind

Anika Paris

or die in their sleep.
But watching my father shrink away
in a rehab hospital
brings it home:
indifferent nurses
giving him pills
trying to quiet him down
assuring him he'll be okay
while he fights to be heard
to mean something—
hoping to be big enough
the world will stop without him.

LAS NENAS

Éramos tres
Saura Vilia Beth
adolescentes llamadas
—N-E-E-n-a-as—
porque aun teníamos madre.

Yo era la mayor,
la que vendía flores
en los clubes nocturnos
sin decir nada a nadie.

En navidades me compré
un vestido para lucirlo
entre los chicos
que venían a rondarnos.

Escondiendo mi tesoro
en el ropero de espejo,
no engañaba yo a mi madre.

¿Como no iba a saber?
si extasiada yo posaba
ante la magia del imagen
con aire sofisticado,
ya transformada en mujer.

Pero éramos tres
Saura Vilia Beth
debutantes de la vida
con pestillos y amoríos
de cachorros. Los ahorros
eran míos —¡mas, que bien
se vería Saura y
como luciera Beth!

La conciencia me picaba...
y mi madre, fuente
de buenos consejos

que todo lo adivinaba,
nos brindó su parecer:

—Nenas, sean hermanitas buenas
así ninguna se ofende
y lo disfrutan las tres.—

—Pero mami...el trajecito
es tan fino. Mira,
ni si fuera de papel.
A Beth le quedará corto
y a Saura hasta los pies,
y yo: maniquí de vidriera.
Ningún vestido sirviera
para dos, menos a tres.—

Fué así que del tingo al tango
el ruedo, en la tarde del domingo
se subía para Saura, el sábado
por la tarde se bajaba para Beth,

y en la noche, era mío,
mi tesoro, ya marchito—
y del tiro aprendimos a coser.

—¡A sobaquina adolescente!—
dijo el sastre, que ya olía
mi precioso trajecito de Chanel,
fina piel de busca-novios.

Más por él, fuimos hermanitas buenas,
y por él, ya dejamos de ser
—¡N-E-E-n-a-as!—

LITTLE GIRLS / LAS NENAS

We were three
Saura   Vilia   Beth
the cutest, poorest
adolescents known as one:
¡Ne-e-n-a-as!
because we still had Mother.

I was the oldest,
I sold flowers in the night clubs,
without telling a soul.

At Christmas I bought myself
a dress so I could show off
in front of the boys,
who would hang around flirting.

Stashing my treasure
in the armoire
I didn't fool my mother one bit.
How could she *not* know
as I'd pose ecstatically
before my reflection,
putting on sophisticated airs,
magically transformed into a woman.

But we were three
Saura   Vilia   Beth
debutantes of life
with "steadies" and puppy loves.
The savings may have been mine,
but how pretty Saura would look
and oh how Beth would shine!
My conscience pricked me...

and Mother, fountain
of good counsel,

who left nothing unsaid,
proffered her opinion:

"Girls, be good sisters
that way no one will be hurt
and all three of you will benefit."

"But Mami...the little dress
is so delicate. Look,
it's as if it were made of paper.
On Beth it would be too short
and on Saura, way down to her feet,
while on *me*: a perfect mannequin.
No one dress could fit
two of us, let alone three"

That's when we three learned to sew.
The hem went from pillar to post:
on Sunday afternoon it was raised
for Saura, Saturday afternoon
it was lowered for Beth,

and at night it was mine,
my treasure, withered and worn.

"Adolescent B.O." said the cleaner
turning away his nose
at my precious little Chanel, second skin
matching my alluring spit curls.

Yet because of the dress we remained
loving sisters, and because of it
we stopped being *¡n-e-e-n-a-as!*

Nenas: *"little girls!"*

HERMANAS

Medía yo cinco pies
cinco pulgadas
mi hermana cinco-ocho

Ella me llamaba enana

Yo era más como mi padre
era trigueña
ella era rubia

Ella me llamaba prieta

Yo nací en Puerto Rico
ella en el Norte
yo hablaba con acento

Ella me llamaba gaga

Ella era quieta
y yo viva de palabras
traté, traté, y tanto traté

que un dia confesó:
¡Estoy honrada de ser tu hermana!

Anita Vélez-Mitchell

SISTERS

I was five feet
five inches tall
my sister was five-eight

She called me midget

I took after my father
I was brunette
and she was blonde

She called me swarthy

I was born in Puerto Rico
she in the USA
I had an accent

She said I stuttered

She was a quiet kid
and I was full of words
I tried and tried and tried so hard

that one day she confessed:
I'm proud to be your sister!

(translated by Anita Velez-Mitchell)

A STRING OF PEARLS

My Aunt Sally taught me to dance the lindy
when I was a kid. We would practice in
the living room of her honeymoon apartment
on the upper Westside, the victrola blaring
Glenn Miller's "String of Pearls," her own
flapping against her blue back-buttoned
sweater, the glasses and dishes in the drain
paradiddling as we hopped up and down
across the kitchen's green linoleum, past
the dining room, through the living room,
and down the spine of the long hallway.

The women would gather at Aunt Sally's
in the evening after work, and dance and
dance well past the hour of pain, dance
late into the nght, before walking home
to their empty apartments and empty beds.

Besides my grandfather, who was past
his prime, the war had taken all their men—
including Uncle Ralph who was in the Navy—
planting them in strange ports and rain-
drenched jungles with secret names,
dressed them like foliage, faces tarred
and bodies leafed with Pacific palm fronds—
a strategy devised at Birnam Wood,
though with no clearing to advance as one.

At Sally's they would clear the floor, move
the furniture against the wall, and dance
to Frankie, Bing, and Perry Como, who'd cajole
them to be patient, remain faithful, *till
apple blossom time*—though all the men
left behind were *either too young or too old.*

I enjoyed the company of my aunt's friends,
observing their daily rituals brought on

by rationing, watching them transform
their legs with makeup and a penciled
black seam up the calf, painting their nails
and lips blood-red, as if to shoo away
distress signals from overseas. Most of all,
I liked to watch them dance together—
awkwardly at first, breasts brushing against breasts,
then more gracefully as the war wore on.

I loved dancing with my Aunt Sally,
who would guide my arms like a puppeteer
to get my body moving in the right
direction, then fling me up in the air, and
down between her legs, up again, over
her left hip, then her right, controlling
my every move, every gesture at a time
when the rest of the world had lost control.

THE DAY MY UNCLE BECAME A REVOLUTIONARY

""*Yo no tiro a matar a mi pueblo.*"
—Carlos Vélez-Rieckehoff
Massacre of Ponce, Palm Sunday, March 21, 1937

He stands by the church, khaki
sticking to his flesh, the rifle heavy
in his hands, wondering what the fuss
is about. He has a job, a place
to sleep, three squares. He sees them
marching down the road, hundreds strong,
nurses and boy scouts in crisp uniforms,
men in mourning, women celebrating
possibilities, white roses in their hair,
their white dresses buoyant in the sun,
children clutching blossoms in their small
hands—*his* people, coming to rally
in the plaza, their voices raised in the song
of the land, their fists in protest.

He will stand firm here, this day,
before this church, before God, before
the lifeless American flag on La Bombera,
the flag he has sworn to protect and
uphold. Otherwise, it is a morning
like all others, sultry with no chance of rain.

Beads of perspiration trickle down
his cheeks and neck. They feel like
Laura's fingertips coaxing back a strand
of hair as it falls in a silent wave over
his brow. He longs to hold her moist
palms to his lips, suck up their salt, but
the order to prepare to fire slices
his thoughts in two, her image falling as
soundlessly as her clothes to the pavement.

Through the open doors of the church he
can hear the Spanish priest lisping Mass,

the congregation responding as one—
only in church, he thinks; out here
in the real world it is each man for himself.

The parade begins to close in—he senses
the tension in the other soldiers.
His bowels start to churn, his mind
to ask the wrong questions. What right
have they to upset his Sunday plans with
their nonsense? This is a day of peace,
a day he would have spent lying
beside Laura on the beach, not standing
here in the blistering heat. The anthem
sharpens into a rhythmic chant—

LIBERTAD, LIBERTAD,
LIBERTAD PARA PUERTO RICO

They keep coming. He stands firm,
gripping his rifle until his hands ache.
They will try to push past him.
He has orders to stop them, to keep
them out of the plaza. He scans the faces
in the crowd and recognizes two of his
classmates from the Academy. And there
is Carla, Laura's friend, and *ay bendito*,
Doña Isabel—what are they doing here?
The prayers from the church grow louder,
insinuating themselves into the chants

LIBERTAD PARA... Padre Nuestro
que estas en... PUERTO RICO

A young woman is shoved
against him by the crowd. He pushes
her back with the side of his rifle.
Her pale eyes hook his—*¡Desgraciao!*—
she hisses the word between clenched
teeth. A lesser man would shoot her,

he tells himself, and be absolved:
in the line of duty, provocation—
all those excuses men like him use
to tame a people, a nation—their
own people, their own nation.

Sanctificado sea... PUERTO RICO
Venga a nos en...PUERTO RICO

The marchers press forward.
"Get back!" he shouts. "You'll get hurt!"
—*¡Sinvergüenza!*—the girl hisses again.
She is so close he can smell
the flower in her hair. Her mouth
is red and full like Laura's. If he were
to move a fraction of an inch lower
their lips would touch and he could
kiss away her disgust. "Get back! *¡Atrás!*"
he shouts again. And again the crowd
presses forward. He feels her breasts
against the backs of his hands. Her eyes,
the color of seafoam, remind him
of his mother's. He feels an unexplained
love for her—this girl who curses him,
who wishes him harm. He wants
to embrace her, to keep her from what
he knows yet does not know will happen.
She is his sister, his lover, his flesh.

He hears gunfire, then screaming. People
try to turn and run, but they are
locked in. They can only move forward
toward the guards. Then more gunfire.
More screaming. The girl's head suddenly
flips back and she begins to fall. He thinks
she has fainted and reaches an arm
around her to hold her up. Her back
is hot, wet. He cannot let go of her

or she will be trampled. Again,
the crowd surges forward, shattering
like glass against the gunfire of the guards.

Those in the front lines fall in rows like
foot soldiers in combat. A young boy
screaming with terror attaches himself
to his leg. He looks down and sees himself.
He hands his rifle to one of the marchers,
lifts the girl's body into his arms, and
turns to face the soldiers. Her blood
bonds them in a wordless pact.

> *Su voluntad aquí en*...PUERTO RICO
> ...*como en el cielo.*

> *Thy will be done in*...PUERTO RICO
> ...*as it is in heaven.*

Yo no tiro a matar a mi pueblo: *I will not shoot my own people.*
Desgraciao: *disgraceful*
LIBERTAD PARA... *Freedom for...*
Padre Nuestro: *Our Father*
que estas en: *who art in*
Sanctificado sea: *Hallowed be*
Venga a nos en: *Thy kingdom come*
Sinvergüenza: *shameless scoundrel*

CRY UNCLE

for Carlos Vélez-Rieckehoff

They say he was a revolutionary
in single-handed combat with contemporary
conquistadores who invaded his island's shores.
They say he was a demagogue, disrupting
non-too-civic councils, hitting hard,
baffling the foe, then running for cover
to the hills in and around Ciales, Novillo,
and points west where Yankee soldiers, lost
in the intricacies of hollows,
underbrush, and overload, deigned to follow.

They say, they say—but what they say is buried
like cloves of garlic deep into the diagonal slits
of my uncle's blue-grey eyes, and what I see
across from me is a mild, bearded, old man who sits
eating quiche at Columbus Restaurant, haunt
of the undaunted: Madonna, Penn, Baryshnikov—
a far cry from revolution, *patria, libertad,*
a far cry from principles and other food for thought.

My uncle's pale grey suit, like one he wore
to his nephew's wedding the night before,
matches his eyes. My mother, on my right, her hands
on her brother's, tries to woo him with a clone smile.
In vain. He sees her coquetry as puerile
next to the manly courage his island demands.

(In the photo my husband later will take,
my mother will lean toward her brother, he
toward me, and I, stalwart as a tree,
try to keep the House of Medina from toppling down—
yes, I, the youngest, am doomed to pillarhood,
rebellion sucked from my bones early on.)

Besides my uncle's suit and his eyes
and the veins straddling tendons

across the backs of his laced hands, another
blueness infiltrates his person, hones his mirth.
It bruises the edge of every gesture,
every word, pares slogans down to sighs.
He turns to me now. But I am dry. Brittle,
Old before my time. No one is left to justify
his failure, to render his lifelong mission holy.

QUÉ TÍO

—para Carlos Vélez Rieckehoff

Dicen que era un revolucionario
mano a mano en combate con conquistadores
contemporáneos quienes invadieron las playas de su isla.
Dicen que era un radical, dando candela,
despistando al enemigo, luego corriendo a
refugiarse en las lomas y los alrededores
de Ciales, Novillo y hacia el oeste
donde los soldados Yanquis, perdidos
en la marana de vegas, matorrales y hojarasca,
se dignaron a seguirlo.

Dicen, dicen—pero lo que dicen está enterrado
como dientes de ajo adentrados en las rajas diagonales
de los ojos azul-grisaceos de mi tío, y lo que yo veo
frente a mí es un modesto viejo barbudo
que está sentado comiendo quiche en el restaurante Columbus,
guarida de los intrépidos: Madonna, Penn, Baryshnikov -
muy lejos de la revolución, patria, libertád—

El traje de colór pálido de mi tío hace juego con sus ojos.
Mi madre, sus manos agarrando las de su hermano,
trata de seducirlo con una sonrisa imitada.
De nada sirve. Él ve su coquetería pueril comparado
con el coraje varonil que exige su isla.

(En la foto que mi esposo tomará luego,
mi madre se inclina hacia su hermano, él
hacia mí, y yo, fornida como un arbol,
trato de evitar que la casa de Medina se derrumbe—
sí, yo la mas joven, estoy destinada a ser baluarte.)

Además del traje y los ojos de mi tío
y los tendones montados a cada lado de las venas
de sus manos entrelazadas, otra
melancolía infiltra su persona, agudiza su regocijo.
Lastima el borde de cada gesto,

cada palabra, los decires acaban en suspiros.
Ahora se vira hacia mí. Pero yo estoy seca. Fragil.
Deslucida antes de tiempo. No queda nadie que justifique
su fracaso, que rinda homenaje a la sagrada misión de su vida.

(Traducción: Anita Vélez-Mitchell)

OLFACTORY

I remember South Hampton
coffeecakes and rose bushes
sea salt crawling up my nose
attic treasures in drawers from summers past
mold from the cellar crashing our party
sitting next to us while we watched cartoons
on the first giant Technicolor screen projector

My Aunt Jane would put us in the back
of her boyfriend Louie's van
on the mattress tied to the floor
We'd hang on for dear life
as we turned every corner
at speeds outside the law
savoring the vanilla dip Carvel cone
catching its sins with our tongues

The Corrigans from next door
applauded my visits, offering me milk and cookies
every time I'd get bored at
my grandparents' bay view cocktail parties
sour liquored breath and cigarettes
stinging the air, decorating their laughter
hovering above my head with jokes
and rhetoric too tall for me

Strange, how in one second I can be catapulted
back through space and time
by the aroma of pastries on Doheny
It's clear as day
that smell, that feeling, that sweetness
of summers still under my skin.

WINGS

It took us by storm
only in books had we seen an airplane.
How could people do as birds do?
It was insane.
A *kite* was a marvel to us at that age—
let alone a plane!
I was ten.

The telegram read:
I'll be flying to Vieques soon,
tell the kids to prepare for a loop-the-loop.
Coming from wild Uncle Frank this was scary,
but exciting.
Days passed and our necks got stiff from peering up at the sky.
Then, one dawn, the thunderous engines roared,
and we watched on the run, this winged armature
try to touch down.

Like a sick bird, it wobbled and flopped,
until it finally landed on our grassy lot.
We ran, screaming, till the pilot emerged
like an outer-space hero in front of our eyes.
We kids were wise:
Uncle Frank had stolen the bird's gift to fly.

We stood there trembling in line,
as he took us, one by one, up to the sky. What a sight!
Down they came, tumbling,
choking, purple from fear,
as they stumbled out of the plane.

At last came my turn.

Soon, we were hundreds of feet in the air.
Desperately, I searched for them past the puffy clouds.
No doubt they would be waiting for me.
Suddenly, I found myself going in circles.

Stop it! Please! Don't! I cried, tears rolling down my face.
That loop-the-loop was a curse, Uncle Frank—
You've frightened the angels away!

We bounced back to earth, he took off his glasses and hood.
Then, hugging me tightly, he said:
The angels, my darling, are here on earth,
They're not way up in the sky,
they are here to guide us and help us through life.
Mamá is an angel, and so is Papá.
Your teacher, your friends, your neighbors!
The world is teeming with angels
and you too are an angel. Never forget that.

And so are you, Uncle Frank, I smiled.

Then the chorus of angels burst out on the ground.
Thank you, thank you, Uncle Frank!
We'll always remember this heavenly flight.

Gloria Vando

AFTER THE 1916 HURRICANE DEVASTATES AÑASCO, MY GRANDFATHER, PACO VÉLEZ, JOINS THE UNEMPLOYED

1.
"Go," she says, "my sister Ana's husband
will help us." And so he boards the ferry
for Vieques, in a pristine white suit and
Panama hat worthy of his station.

His brother-in-law sits behind his huge
mahogany desk and laughs. "You are coffee,"
he scoffs. "We are sugar. One catastrophe
and you're wiped out. We endure. Sugar is
king. And now you come to me hat in hand.
Bueno, hermanito, here we work our
way up. Juan will show you what to do."

Paco follows Juan's extended finger
to a mountain of sugar bales. "I throw,
you catch," a worker shouts down to him from
the mountaintop, "then place it over there."

Paco waits below, arms outstretched, ready
to receive the insult. The 100-pound
bale knocks him flat. He stands up, shakes the dust
off, puts his hat back on his head, and tries
again. And again he falls. He makes no
connection between his lot and that of
Sisyphus. After the sixth assault, he
tips his hat, bows slightly, and walks away.

But how can he go home? How can he *not?*
He sees his pregnant wife in a chair—
no, by the window—no, pacing back and forth,
waiting for her salvation to burst through
the door—*Ah, the sight of him!* She will run
to him, throw her arms around his lean chest,
kiss him full on the lips—and ask how he fared.

2.

She sits and waits now, but not for him. He
has vanished from her life. A notice in
El Tiempo exonerates her of all
his debts—a love letter, of sorts. His white
coat washes ashore; his hat floats in and
out with the tides.

When her child comes, she calls
her Ana Vilia, after her sister
and the nymph in "The Merry Widow" waltz—

> *Vilia, O Vilia, I've waited so long;*
> *Lonely, so lonely, with only a song.*

LAME DUCK

Titi Ana never walked.
She married a rich man
whose chauffeured Hudson
transported her through
much of her life. Diminished
in energy and muscle tone,
she grew in girth.

Don Pepe found a slimmer,
younger companion to sit
beside him in the rear seat
of his new sedan and nod
her head to the *jíbaros* who
tended his sugar plantation.

I was twelve when I visited
my grand aunt for the first time.
Her now modest surroundings
serving her well, as she
shuffled from room to room.

Though her drinking water was
no longer imported from France,
it still had to be boiled and
filtered and she'd balk as
I drank glass after glass to quench
my thirst after jogging up and
down the dignified streets
of Santurce in the 90° heat.

A New Yorker on holiday
I was not attuned to the ways
of the "gentry": I giggled, sang,
sunbathed, quaffed water, and
in the long run, preferred
to hang out with her *sirvienta*,
a young girl closer to my age
than any of my haughty relatives.

Titi Ana sighed a lot. Maybe
for her lost life, probably for
what she saw as the degeneration
of my generation, annoyingly
progressive and resistant
to authority. She died soon after,
amid the laughter and chatter
of the changing world around her,
died quietly, in her favorite chair.

CAFÉ CON LECHE

My grandfather sits at the round kitchen table
overlooking the third Avenue El. But first he
has washed his hands, dried them with one
of the brown paper bags he stores. He washes
his hands every 17 minutes. He is a pharmacist
a failed physician: cloth towels are unsanitary.

He reaches for the milk steaming on the stove,
slowly pours it into his cup. *Nata* floats like
a cataract to the surface. From the ice box
he retrieves the extract of coffee, a potion
he brews first thing every morning, when
the chase lets up long enough for him to awaken,
and, ill-humored and afraid, he makes his way
to the kitchen, night clinging to the shades
and to his eyelids. He grinds the beans
to a fine powder and spoons it into the *colador*.
Over this, he pours boiling water, one ounce
at a time, coaxing the moistened grounds
to the center of the cloth funnel, where the water
washes them clean, unlike my grandfather's sins.
A deliberate process. My grandfather is patient.

After the brew becomes thick and black,
he chills it in a glass jar and returns to his bed,
anticipating joyous encounters with blonde
blue-eyed angels who look remarkably like
my grandmother when he first laid eyes on her
and lost his head and his heart and his wife
and their nine children—anything, everything,
to make her his own. For better. Or for worse.

My grandfather sits at the round kitchen table.
He pours hot milk into his cup, then adds
a shot-glass full of coffee. The dark forbidden
fragrance invades my senses. I watch
as he stirs in the sugar, the aroma turning
heavy, more tempting with each spoonful.

I butter a slice of plain white bread, fold it,
and wait. My mouth mirrors his pleasure as he
takes his first swallow and sighs contentedly
at this exclusive adult pursuit. I wait, patient
as a small pup, until he offers me his cup—

And before he can balk at the butter, I dunk
my bread into his coffee, bringing
the dripping treat to my lips. The liquid warms
and sweetens my mouth and throat, the salt
of the melted butter rouses my entire body,
blurring my senses for anything less.
I watch the iridescent globules of butterfat
rise to the surface. I am possessed.

---

café con leche—*coffee with milk*
nata—*milk film*
colador—*cloth strainer*

Gloria Vando

ABUELITA HAD A DIRECT LINE TO GOD

no *curas*, no priests to intercede
on her behalf. Just the two of them
on a first name basis: Diós y Lucila.
What does the clergy know about life?
she'd ask. *They tell us to have children,
but do they help with the dishes, the rent?*

My grandparents cared for me
while my mother hung upside down
from a circus trapeze—the only job
that paid enough to feed her large family.
My grandfather, a pharmacist who
spoke no English, was reduced to
selling pharmaceuticals door to door.

Each night Abuelita would read me
a story in Spanish before tucking me in.
I would ask for her *bendición*, her blessing.
She would say, *Diós te bendiga, mi hijita,*
kiss me on the forehead and tiptoe out.
It was a ritual I craved. Even in boarding
school—I would ask and I would receive,
Diós te bendiga, mi hijita, echoing
in my memory and in my dreams.

I was in college, studying philosophy,
when I came home one day eager to share
my new discovery: There is no God!
¡Ay, Madre santísima! Abuelita cried,
and locked herself in her room.
That night, as I had done every night
of my life before falling asleep, I
called out, *Bendición, Abuelita*—
and waited, and waited, for her reply.

Diós te bendiga, mi hijita: *God bless you, my child*

110

THE LANDSCAPE OF MY HEART
—*for Ellen*

Death is not the greatest loss in life. The greatest loss
is what dies inside us while we live.
                    —Norman Cousins

In the landscape of skies
in the indigo blue
that bends day into night
you are

In the arms of summer
in this birth month of June
in the stillness of yesterday
I'll remember you

You once flesh and bone
now embered gold
pollinating your garden of dreams
dusting the eyelashes of your children
your children's children

In the seascapes of Maine
on the shoulders of the Casco Bay
in the curve of its rocks, trees and
crests of new mornings
you'll be dancing

In the perennial beauty of daffodils and tulips
in the valley of Egremont
and each lavendar spring
you'll stay

In the meadow of my life
and each tree-lined memory
forever in the landscape of my heart
you remain

WIND CHILL FACTOR

—for Daisy Rhau

You point to a photo of your family
taken after they fled from North Korea,
your infant mother in her father's arms,
despots pursuing them the way Uncle Sam
pursued my grandparents after confiscating
their power, their land, its yield of sugar
and coffee, iron and ore, giving them
three weeks—always three weeks!—
to relocate. Before the exodus

your mother awoke each morning
in a tepid bath, her sleeping body phased
into a basin of wrist-warm water to lessen
the shock of life, the anticipated march across
the wide divide between privilege and
anonymity—snipers, land mines at every turn.

As a child I awoke to tepid clothes,
my grandmother warming each tiny garment
with her body—my socks running a low
temperature under each arm, my panties
wedged in her cleavage, my shirt sleeves
embracing her neck, her whole body
a conduit of early morning comfort
as she dressed me under the covers,
easing me into the glare of indifference,
then rage, against an alien shade or sound.

She taught me to braid my hair, gathering
the three strands, like warring factions,
between her fingers, plaiting them over and
under and over and under until a perfect braid
emerged, my world in safe and tidy harmony.

Grown up, I wear my hair in a bun, the skill
of my grandmother's hands in mine,
weaving then coiling the long thin braid
into a perfect circle at the nape of my neck,
insulating me, still, against the chill.

Love

O vous qui nous meniez à tout ce vif l'ame,

fortune errante sur les eaux, nous direz-vous un soir sur terre

quelle main nous vêt de cette unique ardente de la

fable, et de quels fonds d'abîme nous vint à bien, nous

vint à mal, toute cette montée d'aube rougissante, et

cette part nous divine qui fut notre part de ténèbres?

—St. John Perse, *"Cronique"*

MARCH

> with its frenzy
>> of wings
>>> touched me
>>>> all over
> it mussed my hair
>> it flipped my mind
>>> and suddenly I became a lover

I forgot all about my long arms and legs
> and left behind the bowl
> of alphabet soup in which
> I would spell my fortune.
In a cock's crow my boobies blossomed
> and the mirror became a lake of desire
> slowly sculpting my longing.
I felt love was everywhere
> a romance around each corner.
> "Hey, Darío, come here! ¡acércate!
> I have a secret just for you!"
But the boys were naive and shy.
> The world at times seemed far
> beyond the rainbow, mostly
> though on this side of the Hudson
> at times.
Suddenly women learned to smile
> and men became most charming!
Luis gave me a chiffon-flowered dress
> for my fifteenth birthday
> I wore it over practically nothing
> and arm-in-arm we went strolling.
It was a spiral of dreams caressing my body
> and I a rosebud walking on air.

Still this *ragazzo* froze,
       his legs wide open
       and said boldly
       "Brava! Sta buona per licare,"
       smacking his lips and
       licking his droolings as if
       I were an all-day sucker.

I liked all the boys—
       most of all, Darío!
But Darío was a choir master and
       all he ever wanted to play was his organ.
Mamá thought Luis was a good catch.
       But Luis was intellectually ambitious
       and would save me his books
       should I go to college....
But we were poor, that is,
       rich without money,
       economic exiles from the island
       sharing everything—
       miseries, joys, burdens, and longings.

One day my eyes caught Emanuel's.
       Gosh he was handsome!
Just like that we exchanged rings
       forgetting he was Jewish
       and I Catholic.
But he returned it next day
       just because I kissed his brother!

Mark was a charmer, faster than Emanuel
       but he wanted to be a movie star
       and wouldn't hold hands
       or put his arms around me.
Then one Sunday I cornered Darío!
We found ourselves alone in church.
       I kissed him with a passion.
       He turned pale, spat, and wiped his mouth
       on his shirt.

Oh, how to wrest the sap from Primavida!
    Innocent lovers
      we'd pass by brushing against each other
      blushingly lowering our eyelids.
And when we met
      oh how we fumbled!
Our hearts spoke faster than our tongues
      flinging our secret world
      into the open!
What to do...
Abandon ourselves like kites to the
      laughing wind,
surrender to nature,
      go wild!

Joy, kids! Come on, let's go....
      It's March!

MARZO
      con
           su
                barullo
                      de aves
                              me palpó
                                    toda,
alborotó mi cabello, trastornó mi cerebro, y de repente
me sentí amante. Olvidé mis brazos y mis piernas largas,
y la sopa de letras donde deletreaba mi suerte. En un quiquiriquí
prendieron mis pezones y el espejo se hizo un lago de antojo
donde cincelar mis ansias. Creí toparme con el amor
por donde quiera, cada esquina me ofrecía una esperanza.

Darío, ven acércate, tengo un secreto sólo para ti.... Pero
los chicos aún castos huían de mí. El mundo estaba más allá
del arcoiris, y a veces más acá del río Hudson. Los seres aprendieron
de pronto a sonreir y ser afables. El vestido de chifón
que me obsequió Luis para mis quince me lo puse
sobre lo estrictamente necesario y nos fuimos de brazo.

Sentía aquel florido traje enroscarse sobre mi cuerpo como una espiral
de sueños caminándome, y yo, una flor abierta de paso. Sin embargo,
dijo un fornido ragazzo: *Sta buona per licare*, ¡mirándome cual si yo
fuera un caramelo y lamiéndose de gusto los labios!

Me encantaban todos, y más Darío. Pero Darío era monaguillo
y se entretenía tocando el órgano. Luis, a quien Mamá
consideraba un buen partido, tenía grandes ambiciones intelectuales
y me guardaba sus libros de colegio, por si acaso...pero
éramos pobres, o más bien, ricos sin dinero. Exilados económicos
de la isla, y lo compartíamos todo, tristeza y alegrías, realidad y sueño.

Miré de reojo a Emanuel. ¡Qué guapo! Así no más nos cambiamos
sortijas. Sin pensar que él era judío y yo cristiana.
Pero me la devolvió al enterarse de que besé
a su hermano. Mark era más insolente y más ardiente que Emanuel,
pero las pretenciones de ser actor de cine lo tenían monosilábico.
No me ofrecía ni su mano ni su brazo. Al fin, un domingo, logré
acorralar a Darío, nos encontramos en la iglesia solos, y lo besé,

lo besé hasta asfixiarlo. Palideció, y luego escupió y se limpió
en la manga los labios.

¡Qué necesidad de apagar ese fuego de primavida!
Amantes inconscientes, nos rozábamos al pasar, sonrojándonos
hasta bajar la vista, titubeábamos, rompía el corazon
antes que el habla, traicionando todo lo que habíamos pensado.
¿Qué hacer? ¡Vamos a dejarnos ir como hace la naturaleza,
abandonarnos a la carcajada del viento como hacen las cometas!
¿Qué hacer? A gozar...vamos, chicos, es MARZO.

COQUÍ OR SOMETHING LIKE IT

If I were a frog
I'd stick out my tongue
and collect all the things that I want

I'd re-define what a "wet willy" is
and sneak one on you
in the middle of something

I'd catch the rain
some pollen
and a little bit of heaven
then leap from fact to fiction
through the looking glass
making sure you were with me
and never look back

ON HEARING MY MOTHER SPEAK LOVINGLY
OF DILLINGER

I've never had the hots for desperados—
they're not the kind of men I'd relish
or, even less, trust with my love or flesh,
recklessly exposing either to casual
(or planned) theft, as to some rare disease
that sneaks up on you and before you know
it has your heart in a stranglehold.
Desperados are cowardly and sly. Mean-
while, your family's bereft, not a dry eye
in the house, and there you are heart-less,
someone's loot to be stashed into a sack,
your fate as sealed as Rigoletto's Gilda.
Or worse, you could be buried in some
far-off site until the heat cooled. Days,
months, years could pass—retrieval takes
too long. Hearts decompose, become
devalued. No. I prefer a thoughtful lover,
one who takes his shoes off, folds his pants
over the back of a chair, removes his
underwear, blankets your warm flesh
with his warm flesh, head to tippy toe—
none of this zip-down-kiss-me stuff and
out the fire-escape window to the gal
next door. A thoughtful man will grab you
in a passionate embrace and breathe life
into you and do all the wild things desperados
do, but he'll say quotable things, words
you can almost believe, words that can
steel you against the tyrannies of the day, against
the onslaught of duty and regimen,
like a good cup of coffee in the morning.

LOST IN MONET'S GARDEN

Among the violets
and the peonies
the water lilies and the light
skimming the surface
with its sleek white tongue,
I look for us.

We danced there once or twice
in another life gone by
you held me then
you let me go
on many starry nights.

And once again I search for
what will always be
and still I always find
I search for joy,
with us in mind.

A FRAGRANT MEAL

"Did you like the roses?" he asked on the phone.
"Delicious," I replied with a satisfied moan.

"Beautiful, is the word, delicious is absurd!"
he said when he heard my response.

"And yet... could be," said he, "let me think.
The roses were pink...and from the word delicate,
one may deduce a poetic scheme.
Ah, deliciously beautiful...I get what you mean."

"That's not at all what I meant," I cut in.
"The roses were pink and delicious. Just think
a dancer out of work is out on a limb—
she's hungry, she's angry, she's mean.
I have no regrets that with a little vinaigrette
they served me a most fragrant meal.
They looked just divine on the plate—
the dozen I ate."

"The dozen roses you ate?"

"Dear man, to you it may sound capricious,
but I'm much obliged, for they were delicious!"

RE-ENCUENTRO

"Too bad...too late
es tarde."

En la playa del amor
orillean las aguas
y la brisa mañanera
murmura tus mismas palabras

"Too bad ... too late
es tarde."

-- Me quieres?
-- Te quiero
-- Entonces...¿por que
lo de ayer?

Rompe el encanto
en el fondo bermejo
del paisaje.

—Te quedas?
—No puedo.

Tu sonrisa enlutada arde
un guiño de lucero
se burla de mis pesares

"Too bad...too late
es tarde."

RE-ENCOUNTER

"Too bad ... too late
es tarde."

At the shore of love
the water's edge
and the morning breeze
murmur the words you say

"Too bad ... too late
es tarde."

"Do you love me?"
"I love you."
"Why then
yesterday?"

The enchantment bursts
in the vermillion depth
of the seascape.

"Can you stay?"
"I can't."

Your mournful smile
is still ardent
a wink of starlight
mocks my sorrow

"Too bad ... too late
es tarde."

(Translation by Anita Velez Mitchell)

Gloria Vando

OUT OF SYNC

God gave the white man clocks,
the Ghanaian time.
—A Ghanaian saying

My watch is simple, black, its spastic
silver hands shove me through the day.

A gift from my husband who claims
I'm slow, straggling like a defiant sheep.

I'd rather think than eat, write than sleep,
I counter, and no matter how I rush,

I am Latina late. He scowls. Fumes.
Wrings his hands. Paces the room.

Nails a railroad clock above my desk,
its face as round as Harpo's, bloated

as W.C. Fields's, clowns who lend me
levity when productivity and praise slow

down. Watch your step, scolds Moonface
every 60 seconds. But I don't want

to be confined to a glass cage, starting
and ending each day at the same place.

I want to zigzag, tango, undulate, unfold,
have a jagged edge to my days (and nights)—

and every now and then, stop cold.

TRAILS OF LOVE

They sit on opposite ends of the room,
of the world,
of breath.
He looking out, she dipping
into a handful of hope.

"It's cloudy again," he murmurs
breaking her comfortable silence
"Yes," she concurs, looking up
as they skim the sky in a parallel gaze
paired for the blip of a second.

Forty years tap dancing
around them like a hurricane,
they, caught in the eye,
dare not reach out.

He goes for a walk.
She revisits herself.
The ghost of what was
still haunting them,
hanging around
forever.

PROFILE OF YOU

Beware!
Gestures deceive
they take on life
they take wing
as a band of crows

a black troop
picking the unmeasured word
from the most sober heart
leaving behind
an undaunted taste of ashes
and grief.

Beware!
The gesture
gives away lies
and undresses truth
at its pleasure.

EL PERFIL DE TU SER

¡Cuidado!
Los gestos traicionan
cobran vida
y se echan a volar
cual bandadas de cuervos

un ejército negro
picoteando la palabra equívoca
en el corazon del más cuerdo
dejando en el acto
un impromptu sabor de cenizas
y agravio

¡Cuidado!
El gesto
traiciona la mentira
y desnuda la verdad
como en un rapto.

Anika Paris

THE WEATHER MAN

Beneath your smooth exterior
a fire's crouched below
filled with unforgiving
thoughts and dreams

The timbre of you
strangely fragile
can turn with the tides
into a hurricane
a monsoon
a violet heat wave
and hang around for hours

I can't predict the precipitation
or when the next storm will appear
I can only wear my emotional overcoat
and wait

SILENT FILM

Black and white you are
like an old time flick
scratched and hard to understand
There's just too much
damn noise

Matinee and evening features
always the same as our days
remain unattended

Your lifeless words my wilted heart
lie somewhere on the cutting room floor

Why not paint some ruby red
or purple hope across my lips
so I can drink the stars
and wrap myself in moonlight.

No...black and white you are
desaturated love
colors gone from everything
we once were

Now washed-out
gray and muted down
you've become intangible
like credits rolling by
so fast they fade away
before your eyes
as surely
as our
story's
coming to its
end.

Anita Vélez-Mitchell

DREAMSONG

They go here
they go there
two enjoying
life as one.

They might stop
at a store
stare at things
they both want.

At the movies
they cuddle
head to head
hand in hand

And they dance
face to face
eyes to eyes
palm to palm

And they dine
in a nook,
and they laugh
sipping wine

And at night
in their bed
they make love
heart to heart.

Lucky day
they pass by
more than once
arm in arm.

Their day done

they go home
pity me
all alone.

Dreaming half
of a dream
singing half
of a song.

HISTORIA DE UNA CARA

Caras de hipocresía
de odio, de temor
de envidia, de celos
de luyuria, de desdén
de alegría
me las ponía
me las quitaba
con ellas jugaba
todo el día
fascinada . . .

me dijiste, al fin,
molesto, que no te gustaba
mi mascarada
lo tomé en serio
y quise que vieras mi cara
Una tras una comencé
a quedar sin ellas
desechando las huellas
de mi vida enmascarada

Llegó el día que esperabas
Esperanzada
la última careta me quité
y ví en mi cara la muerte
ya trazada sobre la cara
de niña que olvidé.

THE HISTORY OF A FACE

Masks of hypocrisy
of hate and fear
of envy, of jealousy
of lust, of disdain
of gaiety.
I would put them on
I would take them off
Day and night
I would play my
fascinating game.

You told me, at last,
upset, that you did not relish
my masquerade.
I took you at your word
wanting you to see my face.

One by one I began
leaving them behind,
discarding all traces
of my masked existence.

The day we waited for arrived.
Brimming with hope
I took off the final mask
and on my face
I beheld death, etched
into the childhood face
I had forgotten.

(Translation by Anita Vélez-Mitchell)

THEN CAME THE RAIN

—for Rick
July 1960-August 2006

I read each word
twisted inside out
as that sinking feeling
rushes up my body

I can hear your voice quivering
behind your secret
Goodbye My Love, you've typed
in the subject box of my email

By the time you read this it'll be too late

They find you Friday morning
after I call the police
who break down your door
while I, on hold, 3,000 miles away
hear the details of your death
So cold, so clinical
So lonely you must have been
waiting there for three days
for someone to come and claim you

I buy plants, soil, fertilizer, grass seed, and rocks
pack them in the trunk of my car
then till the soil of my front lawn
kneading its dried veins with my bare hands
I glaze each new leaf with rain water
dust the flowers
and sow my garden in an emerald mist

I can smell the magnolias
as I bend beneath an August sun
trying desperately to redecorate the world
making it beautiful enough for you
to come back.

NOW

I am ninety-two
at this very moment
it is I poeticizing here with you

Physical reality, vital psychic reality,
consciousness, forgiveness, love
material reality ... All I own!
Not to be confused
with the potential reality
of the unknown.

Will I live to ninety-three
or will I suddenly expire?
Will I come back as a rose
or a thorn?
Poor Anita undone! Still...
life goes on, and on, and on
in this miraculous body I own
at the mercy of the elements—
earth, water, air, fire,
and...oh... men!—
balancing precariously
on the horizon's high wire...
till who knows when.

Anita Vélez-Mitchell

HARDCOVERS

Stroll the sidewalks of New York
and you'll find Manhattan
enlightened with hardcovers.
Like old beggars in distress
they line the busy sidewalks,
beckoning to one's book-wormy
conscience, begging to be read.
I stop to open one at random,
lowering my eyes to the text—

Arise and drink your bliss,
writes Blake, *for everything is holy.*
A book's half-erased spine by TOLSTOY
sighs, open me: *The recognition of
the sacredness of everyman's life is first and only.*
I linger, long admiring the gilt edges,
touching their moldy jackets, knowing
they compress realms of wisdom.

Phrases underlined like authors' eyes
after a night of vigil waiting for the Muse
to sing or sigh, link me to the anonymous lover
of belles-lettres who once held
these creative renderings in her hands.

I too tenderline the touching passages
and highlight the quotable stuff.
I too scribble in margins,
quarreling with the author's vanity,
comparing the earthly with the gods.

I put up a hard bargain for
Colette, Shakespeare, Sylvia Plath,
Cervantes, Dostoevsky, Octavio Paz,
and walk home embracing
these affordable life-works that once
tutored my ésprit and savoir-faire.

I stack the six immortals I've rescued
from the gutter, like steps leading to an altar.
I read from them in intimate prayer,
forging my future from the past.
How can anyone throw such faithful friends away?
Friends come in handy when one
is lonely; especially those who thrive and
must be expert in street-smarts—
like these urchins who refuse to die.

THAT POTATO THERE

Brown and dense
like a used paper bag
stuffed to the rim
with a vagabond's dream
that potato there ...
is lying at my feet.

But I prefer to gaze at the fresh pick of the day.
Peaches and oranges colorfully sweet
applaud me as I parade through Gelson's Market.
Fields of green,
ripe jelly-filled tomatoes,
hot pink radishes and yellow squash
glistening in a man-made dew
catch my eye.

And that potato there...
well, it has no chance in Hollywood—who are we kidding?
They just tossed it aside
like an old dusty box you'd store in the attic—
a box holding secrets
you wouldn't want caught in a Sunday breeze.

Deceptively quiet
beneath that porous surface
is a moonful whisper—
virginally tender and eager to please,
guaranteed to fill you up
long after the garish fruits and vegetables start to fade.

That brown potato
once buried in a mossy sea,
yanked from the arms of its Mother Earth
may not appeal to the naked eye,
but always gratifies a lover
with a hungry heart.

Telling Stories

MY FOUNTAIN OF YOUTH

As a native Boricua
I'm proud of my
historic past,
when our then
Governor of Puerto Rico
Don Juan Ponce de León
left San Juan
in search of
the fountain of youth—
and discovered Florida
a land of freedom and truth.

Now I know how he felt
when he sailed the high seas
guarded by his Taíno natives
who loved and protected him.
In my dream it is my doctors
who take me on this evocative
adventurous journey to my
own fountain of youth.

I dream that these super-
heroes are leading me
across the vibrant seas
of Antioxidants.
My caravels teeming
with spirulina, broccoli,
garlic and onions,
spinach, apples, cherries,
almonds, walnuts, flaxseed,
berries, and other
colorful helpings of those
organic musts.

And for good taste:
basil, sage, oregano, rosemary
and umpteen more of these

antibacterial tasty bites
in the culinary dictionary.
In this expedition
they wisely advise
caloric restriction is wise
to avoid those dreaded
free radicals
those caitiff rogues
who pursue my bio-ethereal
cruise to the fountain of youth.

In unison they sing
ting-a-ling
the land of your dreams
is not so far away:
better mental function
less joint disease
better eyesight
sleep at ease
good digestion
and great sex—
be my guest!
Some sing soprano
others sing bass.

I wake up and to my amazement
I feel ship-shape as if I had
returned from my psychic domain.
As a nonagenarian Hispanic
vegetarian, I must reveal
my avid craving
for rice and beans
and a demitasse
of Bustelo Café.
I don't care what they say.
And a glass of red wine,
I don't think they'll mind.

So, as with Don Juan,
my soulful adventure
deserves an historic spot.

Don Juan's was from
the Caribbean to Florida,
Mine, across
the enteric canal
from mouth to gut.

Sailing...sailing...
to my own kitchen
of beauty and truth.
I'll let the world know
when I set foot
on my own florid
fountain of youth.

DR. FEELGOOD

for Anita Vélez-Mitchell

He gave me a shot
of—was it B12?
I thought I could fly.
Talked my way
into all the embassies
on Fifth Avenue, said
I was a reporter
from Madrid, took notes,
promised to send copies
of my stories. On
the way home I stopped
traffic, lifting my hand
with such authority
cars cringed while I
crossed the street.
B12? He said it was B12,
said he gave it to Kennedy,
gave it to Van Cliburn,
gave it to Eddie Fisher,
even gave it to Marilyn
Monroe, and now
because I was special
and he liked me so much
he was giving it to me.
I thought I could fly.

MEMORIAL DAY

It's 80 degrees this weekend
I've been in a bad relationship
with the moody weather
unsure of what season we're in

It's high noon and I'm sitting out back
still in my bathrobe
Dean and Chris are lying on the grass
looking through binoculars at
the strange object flying in the sky
I've been on the phone since 8:30 A.M.
talking to my family in New York
who are getting rain and a much colder day

Ellen's not getting any better
perhaps weeks even days now before the "cancer"
takes her back to Mother Earth or up to heaven

Last night, I watched *60 Minutes* on television
about *the invasion of carcinogens*
all the while getting stupefied and by using fewer
brain cells than when I'm sleeping

We're planting a vegetable garden on Sunday
tomatoes, cucumber, lettuce, and broccoli
so I can make salad and not be fearful
of the pesticides or chemicals in our food

The Gulf of Mexico is drenched in oil
I'm drinking spring water from a glass bottle
wearing SPF 30 and talking on speaker phone
to avoid a brain tumor

These are not the days I particularly want to remember
Maybe in hindsight everything will seem better
At least there's a warm breeze
and the bougainvillea is laughing
even though I'm not

IN PERFECT KEY

I almost lost my Maple Leaf Rag.
I used to practice it on the piano daily
while Nancy waited for me
listening from our front porch
wanting me to come out and play.
Dad would yell out from upstairs
you missed the E-flat as my fingers
would feel their way around the keys
my left hand flailing about like a pinball
trying to score.

Today my best friend Piper is visiting us
with Gabriella, her seventeen-year-old daughter.
We've come full circle, she says.
We were seventeen when we met at KU
at the Hawks Crossing one Friday in spring.
Piper was wearing her Stevie Nicks skirt
and an infectious smile as large as the
albino boa constrictor around her neck.
We played hacky sack and drank Heineken beer,
talked about our dreams and leaving Kansas,
both of us outcasts in a conservative world
connected by our zest for life.

I sent them off early this morning
on college tours and decided to visit
my piano and my old friend Joplin.
My motor memory has never failed me before,
but today I got lost, stuck at a place I once danced around.
I tried closing my eyes and playing with complete abandon
my aching fingers and ease now dissonant.

You are not as old as you think you are,
Gabriella told us over breakfast this morning,
sounding exactly like our parents, wise beyond her years—
so I refuse to give up.

It took longer than I hoped, and a few Googles to
find the sheet music, find the chords my fingers
once found in the dark, reading each note like Braille.
I still need to practice it again as I did when I was ten.
Nancy won't be waiting outside anymore,
but I'll visit her on Facebook, relive those days in tweets
and instant messages in our newly found high-tech world.

I think I'll play it for my music history lecture on Monday
when we visit the turn of the 20th century, when song pluggers
rode in horse-drawn buggies carrying upright pianos
and selling sheet music out the back to pedestrians.
And barbershop quartets performed live on the streets singing
Sweet Adeline in four-part harmony outside the five-and-dime.
But the boisterous, seductive ragtime was played behind
closed doors in bars, after hours, to whooping and hollering,
its syncopated rhythms too risqué—as we were for Kansas.

I'll play them my Maple Leaf Rag that went on
to sell one million copies and change the face of jazz.
And I'll pretend it's as easy as pie, they not knowing that
amidst my favorite time signature and song,
I'm reclaiming my youth.

REALITY TV

I admit it
I'm an addict
I TIVO shows when no one's looking
and watch them in the middle of the night

I'll only jump in on conversations
with other viewers, incognito,
whispering about the latest episode
over café latte's and French manicures

They've ended for the summer season
Nighttime rolling in at eight
now accompanied by cricket hums
No TV noise to wash out their unforgiving trill

Heard next season's line-up is over the top
with a new show called *Come Fry With Me*
We follow the interviewing and training
of an electrocutioner on death row
and watch a willing participant throw the switch
on a convicted felon
Kind of sheds new light on the meaning of
Final Episode

I refuse to watch...
well, unless there's nothing else on

MY WILL

I have just made my will—my end by fire,
with poems to be read instead of prayers,
and rather than be host to my organic germs,
I'll bow out to the music of De Falla.

I am at ease with my incensed desires.
I am familiar with the tongues of flame.
and shall accept without a spark of shame
this imminent indignity required.

My spirit will take flight in flagrant spires.
The flare within me will consume my flesh.
I want to spray a jubilee of ashes
on this earth: I want to seize the fire,

matching my passion with a superpyre,
and set my world ablaze when I expire.

GROWING INTO LILAC

Three women in lilac saris, their scarves
uncurling in the cool afternoon breeze,
carry their children in their arms beneath
a canopy of jacaranda trees,

their lavender blossoms scribbling love notes
on the clear blue sky. I slow down my car
to savor this moment of intense spring—
and find myself back in Playa del Mar

with my friend Alice, who, after her son
died, painted her daughter's bedroom in swirls
of lilac, dressed her bed with a lilac
spread and, as if to shield her from the world's

sorrows, hung heavy lilac drapes across
her window. I found the color morose—
not quite blue, not quite rose—a muted
display of Alice's unutterable loss.

I was a new mother, then, both too old
and too young for the subtleties of lilac.
Now, my children grown and gone, the color
feels right—fits me like an embryonic sac.

MEDDLING BETTY

Betty Bugle knows too much
at least for the folks on Sycamore Drive
You can't leave your house without
a thin sliver of nose snooped between two rum-
      colored curtains
strangely pointing you in the right direction

Watering the lawn is an historic event
if you ever read her diary
"My Little Cul-de-sac" by Betty Bugle

She's lived there nearly 40 years
watching the Benjamins, Rutherfords, Beckers and Prices
      become parents, grandparents, in-laws
and even widows

Last week the Gaylords bought the house next door
Brick Tudor
4469 Sycamore
red stone praising its white columns
on the market for less than a day because
Bud Benjamin ran off with the kindergarten teacher

The Gaylords are from Texas
Tom, a stockbroker
Lorraine, a housewife
Betty likes their apple red Cadillac and fancy hats
They look like fine people

She bakes and bakes all day long
her famous lemon squares
rained in confectionary sugar and gushed with raspberries
a sweet aroma whisked in the air
all tucked in a red and yellow basket
perched outside their doorstep
welcoming them to the neighborhood

Betty waits
collecting her mail in full view
sweeping the front porch twice that day
weeding her lawn near their driveway
waiting for an answer

Judd and Rose Rutherford, 4462,
the nine-room mansion across the way
crashed their Mercedes last week and were uninsured
Who could believe it? she thought to herself
For goodness sake!
Still she never batted an eyelash when they drove by
always singing a neighborly "hi."

Brandon Becker, 4467, the quarterback, is leaving
for college next week
He's been cheating on his girlfriend
sneaking out the attic window for nearly a year now
meeting up with John Joseph, kissing him under the birch tree
How his parents didn't know is beyond her!
But he's a kind fellow with a Southern drawl
a perfect gentleman always mowing her lawn
moist and shirtless in the hot summer sun
while she sits on her front porch
longing for lust to invite her back
every time she offers him lemonade with mint leaves

The Prices, 4465, went to the Hamptons this year
leaving two months of their unkempt garden behind
The ivy and flowers unchaperoned
dance wildly Judith Jamison style
soaring towards heaven
stretching above
and whirling across the horizon with abandon

But the Gaylords
not gay at all

not a weed out of place
not a dent on the car
Nothing

Friday night 7 P.M. their television's a little too loud
windows recklessly open
curtains flailing in the wind
From the back of his lazy boy
Tom's head slumped slightly to the left
towards the kitchen
with pale yellow lights winking back
as if they knew something
Betty watches in a dead stare
He never moves, he never winces
never laughs

Lorraine seems oddly sterile
walking by with a giant red knife
dunking it into the sink and
blotting it clean with an oversized sponge
washing the black and white counters
in a tick tock motion,
scrubbing and scrubbing
over and over again

She notices she's stained her baby blue dress
curses aloud trying to wipe it out
then rips it over her shoulders
baring her naked truth
she looks up and sees Betty
screams and shuts the light

Betty waits till the noise dies out
locks her doors and windows
and turns down her conscience

The next morning, a whap on the front door wakes Betty

It is earlier than usual
She scuffs her way downstairs
sees her basket and a note on her welcome mat
her name smudged on top:

Dear Betty,
Thank you for your delicious lemon squares.
We ate them all last night and made a mess
of those raspberries. Thought you'd want your
basket back. Perhaps one of these days we'll have tea.
Lorraine and Tom Gaylord

After all the drama
Betty has yet to see them again
Tom's been out of town for months
so she hears

Still, Betty wonders
what she knows
as she goes with the flow of Sycamore Drive

DROUGHT

Luz heard the old woman tell
her mother that if she'd wash
her daughter's face with the first
rain of May she would turn beautiful.

But her mother laughed, saw only
radiance beneath the scars etched
on her daughter's cheeks.
In desperation Luz placed a bucket

in the yard to catch the rains
that were to fall from heaven:
she was ready to submerge herself
in fairy tales, to find herself

a better ending. Through ten days
of unrelenting heat, she waited,
then seven more in which the ground
spoke to her through parched

and injured lips, spoke ugly words
she did not want to hear.
Another week went by,
the empty pail mocking her plight.

Never mind the bucket, she relented,
one cup of rain would do, a few drops
to sooth each ravaged cheek,
to smooth away her shame.

But May was merciless.
It would not shed a tear.

WIDOWED HEART

—September 11, 2001

I guess it started with the coffee.
He used to like the way I made it.
Now, there's not enough milk,
it's too mercurial,
too bitter,
like the words that dripped from our tired tongues.

It was only 7:35 A.M.
The sky with her hands on her hips
stared back at me
as I turned from him toward the window.

The angry door's bark
shoved my heart,
nipped the nape of my neck
and frayed yet another morning.

It was just another Tuesday,
September 11th,
time for Jeremy's school.

I prepared his lunch,
peanut butter clinging desperately
to the butter knife,
tearing the bread.
His little arms wrapped around my thigh—
he didn't want to go.
I buttoned him up with promise,
said everything would be okay.

How could I have known?
It was just another Tuesday.
I opened the window,
aired out the room,
thinking we'd fix it, like we always did,
over dinner.

SARÓ: HER BACK TO THE SEA

Saró imprisoned in her life
looks at her long thin fingers,
stares at the paintings
of Puerto Rican streets and houses
making windows on the stark
white walls of her cell. Her
dead son's smiling photo crowns
the center of the coffee table
with fading joy. The windows
at her back face the sea,
the mirrored wall at her left reflects
the open door to the hall.
She sits in her favorite chair
looking in, day after day, her
opera-length pearls resting against
her beige print blouse. She wears
beige slacks, beige stockings,
beige shoes, a touch of palest pink
on her lips. The door across
the hall remains shut. The gates
to the elevator remain locked,
the windows remain closed against
the sea's scentless and silent breath,
un suspiro contra la muerte.

---

un suspiro contra la muerte: *a sigh against death*

DAISY RAE BLACK

from Jardine's Jazz Club, Kansas City

I couldn't help noticing her at the corner table
taking in song, sipping on tea,
sitting in her white dress with matching gloves,
pillbox hat and cherry-smeared lips

"I'm Daisy Rae Black," she shouts,
I come all the way from St. Joe, Missouri, to hear jazz"
Every Thursday she drives an hour and a half
and stays till the very last note
"I'm 90 years old, and I play a mean organ"

She sits like a question mark
and talks to the band
Their rosy-cheeked friend sings along,
tapping her tiny bent fingers,
swaying to the melodies peeling back the years,
untwisting her fate
so she can breathe again

I imagine her putting on her Sunday best,
filling in the lines where her youth once stood
with baby blue shadow and pink sun blush,
teasing her white sea of bobby-pinned curls,
shining up the past of her patent leather shoes
escorting her diamonds and pearls
and improvising her way back
to *Jardine's*

FRIENDLY FIRE (or the Placenta of Politics)

I remove my boots, raise my arms, and get frisked
for the 57th time since September 11th.
"May I touch you?" asks the uniformed woman.
"Only if you're a healer," I reply. She pats me down
on top and slides her magic wand up between
my legs. I want to say "higher, higher," but this is
no time for merriment, and my aisle seat on this
Southwest flight is quickly moving to the center.

Crowds of curious passengers prance by wondering
what this evil-doer might have up her pant leg.
We, who have been raised with guilt and shame,
blush at our own innocence—we must have
done something to warrant this embarrassment.
Racial profiling? Hardly. I'm blonde and over 60.
Whatever it is, though, it's mea culpa. My mother,
age 90, had her identity stolen along with her cash.

They grilled her at the Newark airport until she
discovered a frayed SAG card buried in a pocket.
Suddenly she was a *persona grata*, a former
movie queen, and they let her on the flight to L.A.
Getting *out* of L.A. is another matter: Angelenos
are all members of SAG. She's still there.
Landed a role in a soap. My daughter Anika swears
that in Los Angeles it's illegal to be over 25,

have an independent thought, and sport real breasts.
But that all changes once you reach 90. Some
of my friends in New York City are still out of work,
their entire lives in rubble. They'd move here
in a hummingbird second—but they're neither
young enough nor old enough to get hired.
Look at the new films: older women reminiscing
about their young selves. What happened
to that vast chasm in between? Age profiling? Gee.

But L.A.'s pretty safe. Who would want to bomb it?
Aside from the Hollywood sign and Mickey Mouse,
there are no significant monuments. Disneyland
has its own woes with safety and credibility, and
it would be a bad P.R. move to bomb the television
stations—if there's no TV, how would the rest
of the country even know L.A.'d been bombed?
Still, there is death in the air. And in the press.

The end is near. The message may be the same,
but the messenger has switched from the derelict
on the corner to the derelicts on Wall Street.
I ask my daughter Lorca if she fears a nuclear
attack on New York City. "Oh, *please*," she says,
"I'm more afraid of being mugged by a drug addict,
getting hit by a speeding biker, or being pummeled
with a brick by some lunatic who's been released

from a mental hospital. *That's* what I worry about!"
But for me, her mother, it's an even split and I'm not
sure which is worse: to be nuked in one instant by
an unseen, unknown terrorist; or to be terrorized daily
by an economy that, in one breath, says we're broke
and, in another, exhorts us to go shopping.

SAG: *Screen Actors Guild*

DISCOVERING GEHRY

Frank Gehry's Disney Center, downtown Los Angeles

On Grand Street
Martha Graham's
in a pirouette
her mercurial skirt and scarf
swirling in the tempestuous undertow
of winter
her silvery limbs
reaching for Centauri
bidding for applause
in the smokey sunset

I am drawn to her
pulled out of my seat
like dust off a dandelion
fertile
I must touch her
take her in
I'm in awe of her beauty
her strength
her poise
as I watch her take her final bow

STICK FIGURES

Los Angeles: 24 September 2005

We march down 8th Street to the Courthouse,
my dusted CNVA button once again on my lapel,
my youngest child's hand in mine, waving
our freshly made signs with gusto.
Mine: BRAHMS NOT BOMBS (though
Brahms has been long forgotten), Anika's:
BRING BACK MONICA LEWINSKY
(mere child's play compared to this),
FUCK BUSH, screams my high school chum's
(an ordained minister, she's rightly pissed).
We shout and ululate alongside Asians,
dancing Latinos, Blacks, Native Peoples,
Palestinians in smaghs, veterans in wheelchairs,
young children perched on their dad's shoulders,
teenagers bearing witness and hand-lettered signs:
I'M TOO YOUNG TO VOTE
& TOO YOUNG TO DIE!
BUSH SUCKS!
MAKE LEVEES, NOT WAR!
Eleven white-clad college students span the street,
each holding up one black letter of an
imperative message to Congress and the world:
I   M   P   E   A   C   H   B   U   S   H
On the sidewalk, a young man and woman
on stilts, their bodies like stick figures
floating above the crowd, wave their arms
in time to the beat of the drum corps.
Quite spontaneously we break into the familiar
NO MORE WAR! NO MORE WAR!
And, for no apparent reason, except that I'm here
with my daughter and I've marched for peace
so many times before, I burst into tears.

—for Anika and Nancy

POLLOCK-TICKS

Please don't go Pollock on me
You're hard enough to understand as is
with that thick accent
and baggage you wear around your neck
like a noose
blaming God for every wrong detail
a skip in a hemline
a squawking black bird
electric malfunctions
and even bad gardeners

Life is short
and yes we are too
but Jesus should just stay glued to the dashboard
of a Plymouth's fury
and not plague you every time
something goes wrong.

GUERNICA

—for Michael Montel

Could he have imagined
when he wept on canvas
showing the open wounds
of his native soil and flesh
that someday someone
in a country out of range
would transcribe his horror
into stitchery? Yet there it is,

highlighted in the window
of this fancy East Side store:
a massacre in miniature,
stenciled for dowagers
to stitch in shades of gray
while viewing newer wars
in living color.

Farther down Fifth Avenue
Father Berrigan and a few
of his disciples bear witness
on the steps of St. Pat's Cathedral,
leaning wearily across
dead centuries as they
spread the blood-stained word
            thou shalt not kill
in (this time) Cambodia.

Uptown, in the barrio,
a rat-gnawed baby screams.

And somewhere in between
as though to round off
this American joke
a tacit people, unseeing, unseen,
transform Guernica
into needlepoint.

AROUND THE CORNER

I untie the red ribbon
open the package and
there's nothing
my hand mirror
suddenly cracks
my singing canary
died just a moment ago
a shadow clouds the world
from my eyes
a wingless angel plucked
the sunflower of my burning flesh
and an environmental virus suddenly
polluted the horizon
It's one of those days
when I get a fake coin
the mad girl passes by
laughing her heart out
today, even my verses don't rhyme
and I'm not recognized by my brother
Yeah...it's a day when
no one knows who I am
not even I, myself
It's one of those days
in which I lose my soul
around the corner.

A LA VUELTA DE LA ESQUINA

Deshago el lazo rojo
abro el paquete ... y nada
mi espejo de mano
se astilla de repente
mi canario cantor expiró
hace un instante
una sombra nubló el mundo
de mis ojos
un angel sin alas tronchó
el girasol de mis carnes ardientes
y un virus ambiental de repente
apolilló el horizonte. Hoy
es un día de esos en que
me dan una moneda falsa
pasa la niña demente
riendo a carcajadas
hoy hasta mis versos no riman
y mi hermano no me reconoce
¡Vaya!... que es un día en que
nadie sabe quien soy
ni yo misma lo sé
un día de esos donde
a la vuelta de la esquina
pierdo mi alma

THE DAY BEGAN AS USUAL

> *I cannot remember everything*
> *I must have been unconscious most of the time*

Jogging through a tony suburb of the city,
I tune in NPR's tribute to Dietrich Bonhoeffer,
that brave soul who plotted Hitler's death
("tyrannicide as an act of repentance," he
termed it), before escaping to the States and then
returning to Berlin to face his own death—

> *The day began as usual,*
> *Reveille when it was still dark...*

and as I round the corner of this Midwestern
fairy tale—*barrio* it is not—my iPod
switches abruptly—like a warning—to AM,
and a commercial for Terminix insinuates
itself again and again into Schoenberg's
text. Terminix—guaranteed to rid
the world of unwanted roaches, rodents,
vermin (as a downtown guard referred to
the homeless seeking refuge from sub-zero
nights in the lobby of his bank, spraying
them with a new-and-improved tear gas
that spares the furnishings)—Get out!

> *"Get out!"*
> *They came out. Some very slowly;*
> *The old ones, the sick ones;*
> *Some with nervous agility...*

Terminix!—AM's final solution—guaranteed
(or your money back)—to rid you of all
the undesirables civilization, in its infinite
wisdom and mercy, seeks to exterminate—
and I, like that lone survivor, keep running,
running, wondering if I can escape
before the noxious gases of Terminix

Gloria Vando

catch up with me, a *cucaracha* on the loose.

> *Much too much noise!*
> *Much too much commotion!*
> *And not fast enough!*

I think back to the Great Depression when
that generation would reach out
to people down on their luck, offering them
a place to sleep in the barn, a cup of hot
soup on the back porch steps, a day's
labor—a job often invented on the spot.

> *Abzahlen!*
> *One, two, three, four—became faster*
> *and faster—so fast that it finally sounded*
> *like a stampede of wild horses—and*
> *all of a sudden in the middle of it*
> *they began singing the Shema Yisrael!*

Shema! Hear these words! And thou
shalt teach them diligently unto thy children.

I run faster and faster, chasing my shadow
up and down the long, meandering, tree-
lined drive that twists and turns to greet
itself again and again in a narcissistic embrace,
like a serpent before it swallows its own tale,
always with the same delirious ending.

170

(from "Heroes and Villains," a poem in three parts)

Italics from Arnold Schoenberg's "A Survivor from Warsaw."

Shema Yisrael: *a Hebrew prayer recited daily and the last prayer to be uttered before
death. It is a lyrical declaration of faith, beginning: "Hear, O Israel: The Lord our
God, the Lord is One!" (Cf., the Apostles' Creed and the Nicene Creed.)*

PONDERING THE EXISTENCE OF GOD
AND OTHER THINGS

When I die
I know I'll find
all those socks I lost
every time I did the wash

I know that's where they are
in heaven
along with all my friends in party hats
blowing whistlers
and laughing at the insanity
we mortals struggle over year after year

Insignificant things, like
traffic jams and root canals
multiple choice and pelvic exams
hang nails and late fees and
screaming at the automated voice system
praying for a human

Yet somehow
most people have no problem accepting
what they can't see:
God, Angels, the Holy Spirit
and missing socks

Two go in and only one comes out
Nobody knows why
Nobody even asks
after moving all their furniture around
and finding nothing

So all I really know is
when I finally meet my maker
I'm praying for two things
one, that he's good looking
and two, that he has all my socks

Gloria Vando

BROWN OUT or
NO POWER TO THE PEOPLE

It's 108; heat index 128.
She parks her SUV under a tree
and retreats to a warm mint julep
and *The L.A. Times*,
her only source of news.
Photos of firemen carrying
baked octogenarians out of
their apartments on stretchers
hog the front page of the paper.
On page eight, 10,000 tilapia
float belly-up off the coast
of Long Beach, their cold blood
having reached boiling point.
In Florida fishermen flinch
from the poisonous acids
invading their nets. Skin from
their hands and arms mingles
with the dying coral, dead crabs.
In the hot house the orchids gasp
for water every few hours.
Her lawn is burnt to a brittle ochre.
She grabs a power bar and wakes
the children, sprawled wet
and naked on the back seat.
They follow her lantern's eerie circle
through the breathless night,
searching for redemption, forgiveness,
and incandescent light.

SUBURBAN SUICIDE

Who am I not to let that Indian woman dig through
my recycling bin week after week to sell off
the bottles of wine that we drank?
Who I am to tell my neighbor not to park
his ugly broken-down van in front of my house?
I moved to a suburban neighborhood
thinking it would be far enough away
from the noise, the chaos, and realities
I didn't want to see.

I've been called a "pedigree," a "princess," by friends
who've had it harder, as if I'm unaware
of the trouble our world is in.
Still, I find I'm unable to build that white fence
around my yard high enough to hide the truth,
high enough to blind my heart.

Just a hiccup north, we're deep in Mexico,
all the men standing on corners begging for work.
Slightly west, a quiet neighborhood I wouldn't
want to walk in alone at night.

This is our new world, my new world,
a new America, the land of opportunity.

THE ESSENTIAL POEM

Plato,
you had your excuses
for knocking poets
off their pedestals.

Too early in life
you knocked yourself off
to join the path
of reason
ill-fated Socrates
had furrowed for you.

But poetry,
a trunkless wild vine
that would rather lie
in the hay and look up
at the stars in lovers' eyes,
possessed you.

So you grew,
like a wisdom tooth in
history's mouth,
not knowing your Ideal
was the "essential poem,"
destined to gush forever
in the primeval fountain
of man's soul.

CONTRIBUTORS

ANIKA PARIS was born in Corpus Christi, Texas, and has been playing piano, writing songs, and singing and performing since the age of seven. She blames her muse on the nurturing environment she had growing up with a symphonic conductor father and a poet mother. "I am literally a hybrid of the two, but my brother and sister told me I was the milkman's kid!" As a singer/songwriter, Anika is the recipient of ASCAP's Abe Oleman Scholarship (Songwriters Hall of Fame). Her songs are published with Universal Polygram and Warner Chappell, and featured in major motion pictures and on soundtracks. She has released three solo CDs, is the only female composer for WB Telepictures with songs on such popular shows as *Ellen DeGeneres, TMZ, Oprah, American Idol, Sex in the City* and many more. She has been a musical guest on *Late Night's Craig Kilborn, Latin Explosion* (Christina Aguilera & Ricky Martin), toured the U.S., performed for the Royal Princess of Thailand, and had the great honor of sharing the stage with legendary Stevie Wonder, John Legend and John Mayer in a benefit concert. Anika has recently composed the score for the Off-Broadway production, *The Judas Tree*, and with writing partner Dean Landon, the Taíno musical drama, *Temple of the Souls*, which premiered in NYC in 2012. She has taught performance and songwriting at Musicians Institute in Los Angeles the past ten years and her book, *Making Your Mark in Music: Stage Performance Secrets*, was published by Hal Leonard in 2011. As a poet her work has appeared in *The Kansas City Star, Chance of a Ghost* (Helicon Nine Editions), *Poetic Voices Without Borders II* (Gival Press), *Soft Blow Poetry, Spillway, The Mom Egg* (Half Shell Press), and others.

GLORIA VANDO was born in New York City—the first member of her family to be born stateside—and educated there and in Amsterdam, Paris, and Texas. Her first book of poems, *Promesas: Geography of the Impossible* (Arte Publico Press), won the Thorpe Menn Book Award and was a finalist for the Walt Whitman Award. Her latest book, *Shadows & Supposes* (Arte Público Press), won the Alice Fay Di Castagnola Award and the Latino Literary Hall of Fame's Poetry Book Award. Her poems have appeared in many magazines and anthologies, and on the Grammy-nominated *Poetry on Record: 98 Poets Read Their Work 1888-2006.* She is the recipient of the 2009 Poetry Award from El Instituto de Puerto Rico, NY; the first Kansas Arts Commission Poetry Fellowship; two Billee Murray Denny Prizes; a *River Styx* International Poetry Award and others. She is publisher and editor of Helicon Nine Editions, for which she received the CLMP Editor's Grant and the Governor's Arts Award (Kansas). She is also a contributing editor to the *North American Review*. In 1992 she and her husband, Bill Hickok, founded The Writers Place, a literary center, library and art gallery in Kansas City, Missouri. They now live in Los Angeles, where they are on the board of Beyond Baroque, a literary center in Venice.